Beautiful Beasties

Exploring Horror and Fauvism through AI Art

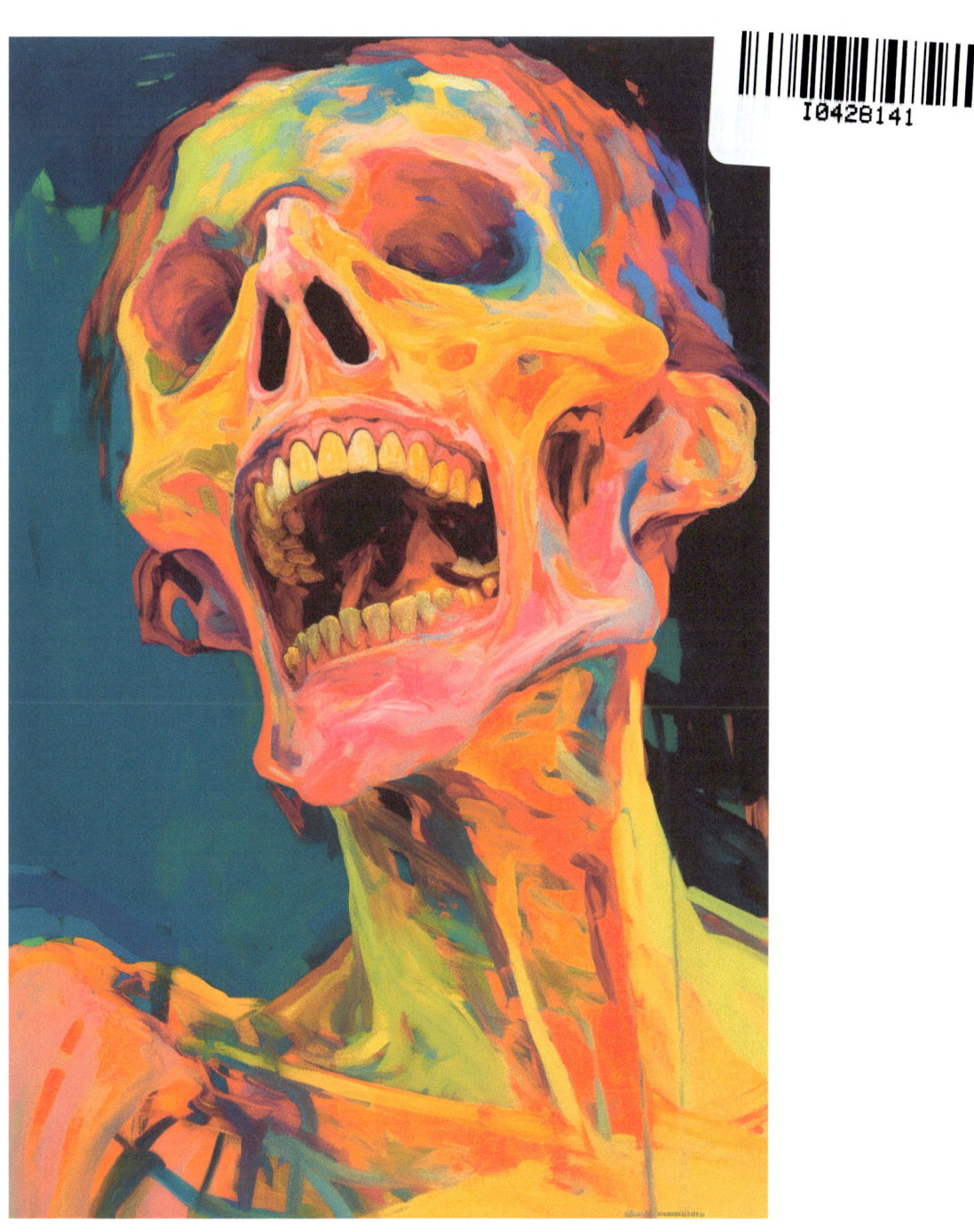

by Lauren McDonagh-Pereira

🌐 laurenmcdonaghpereira.com

🐦 @LAMPphotography

📷 @LAMPphotography.tez

📌 @LaurenMcDonaghPereiraPhoto

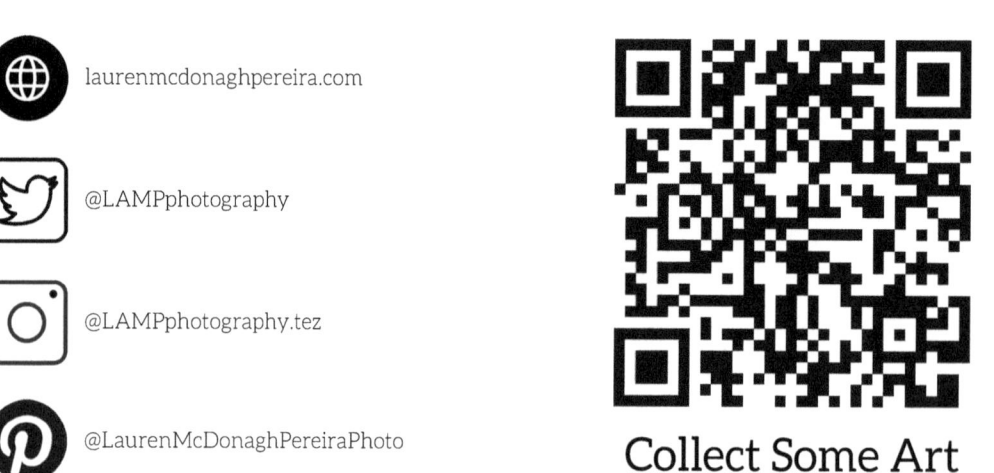

Collect Some Art

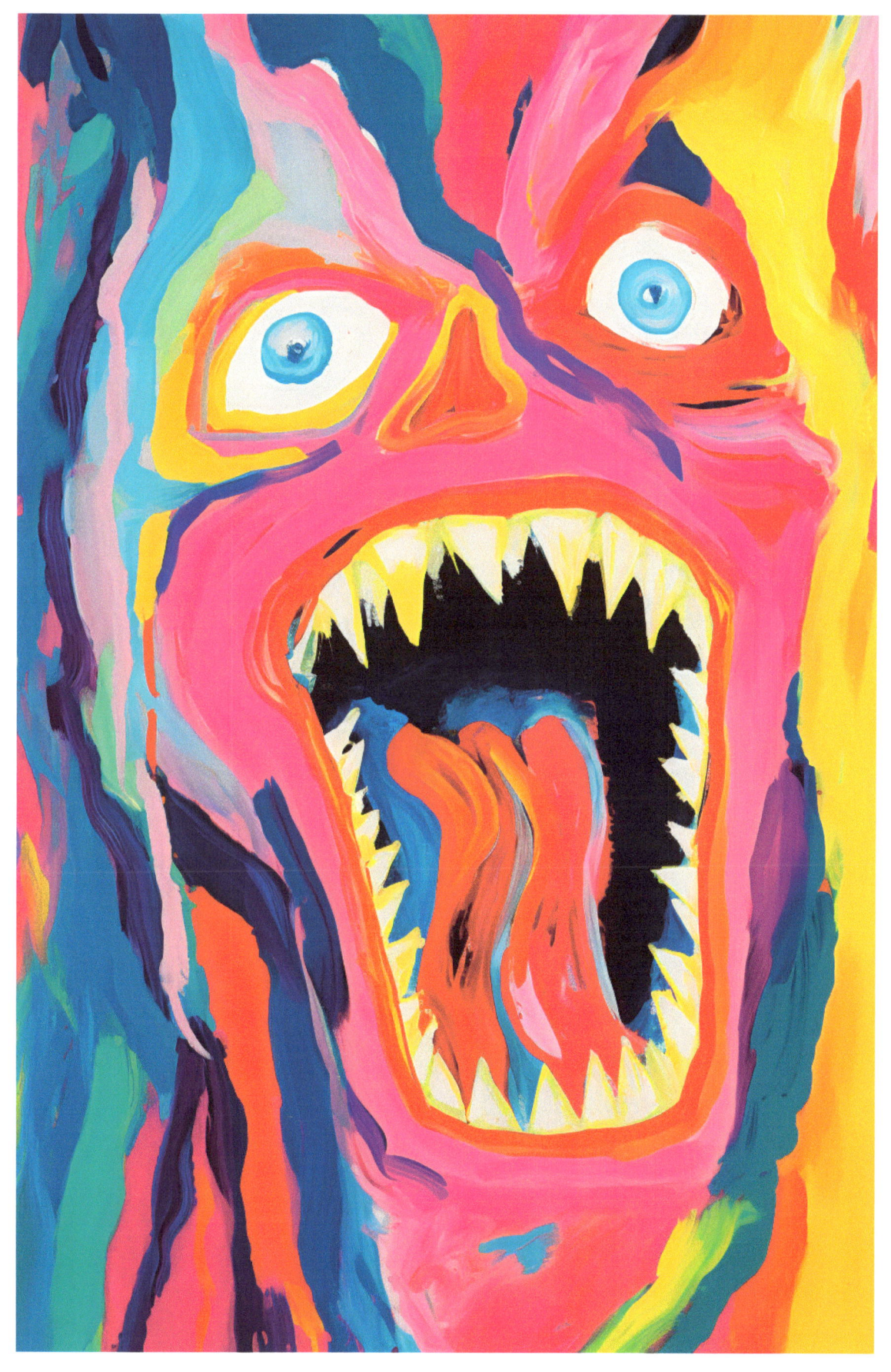

Abyssal Muse

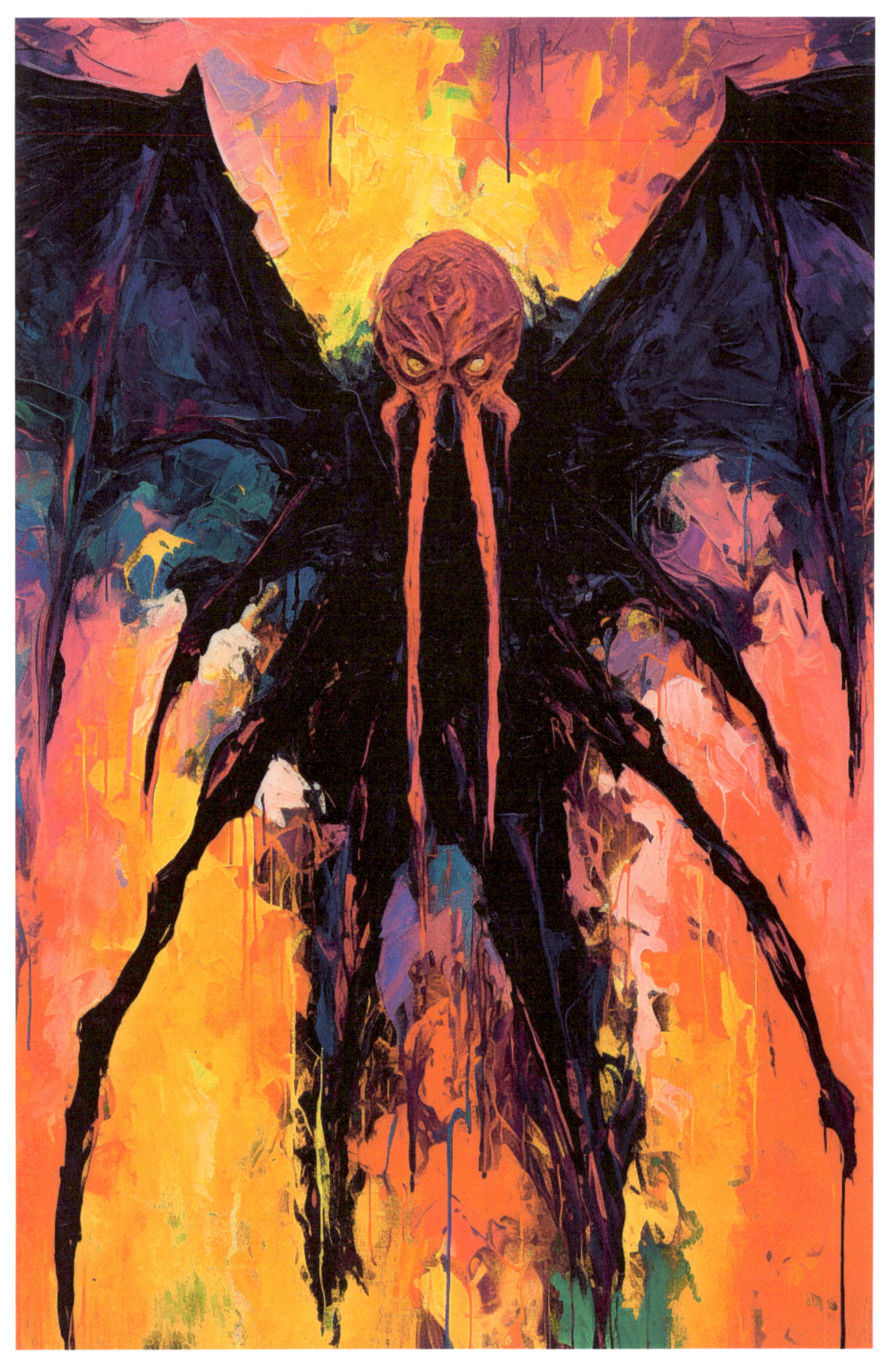

Spectral Mirage

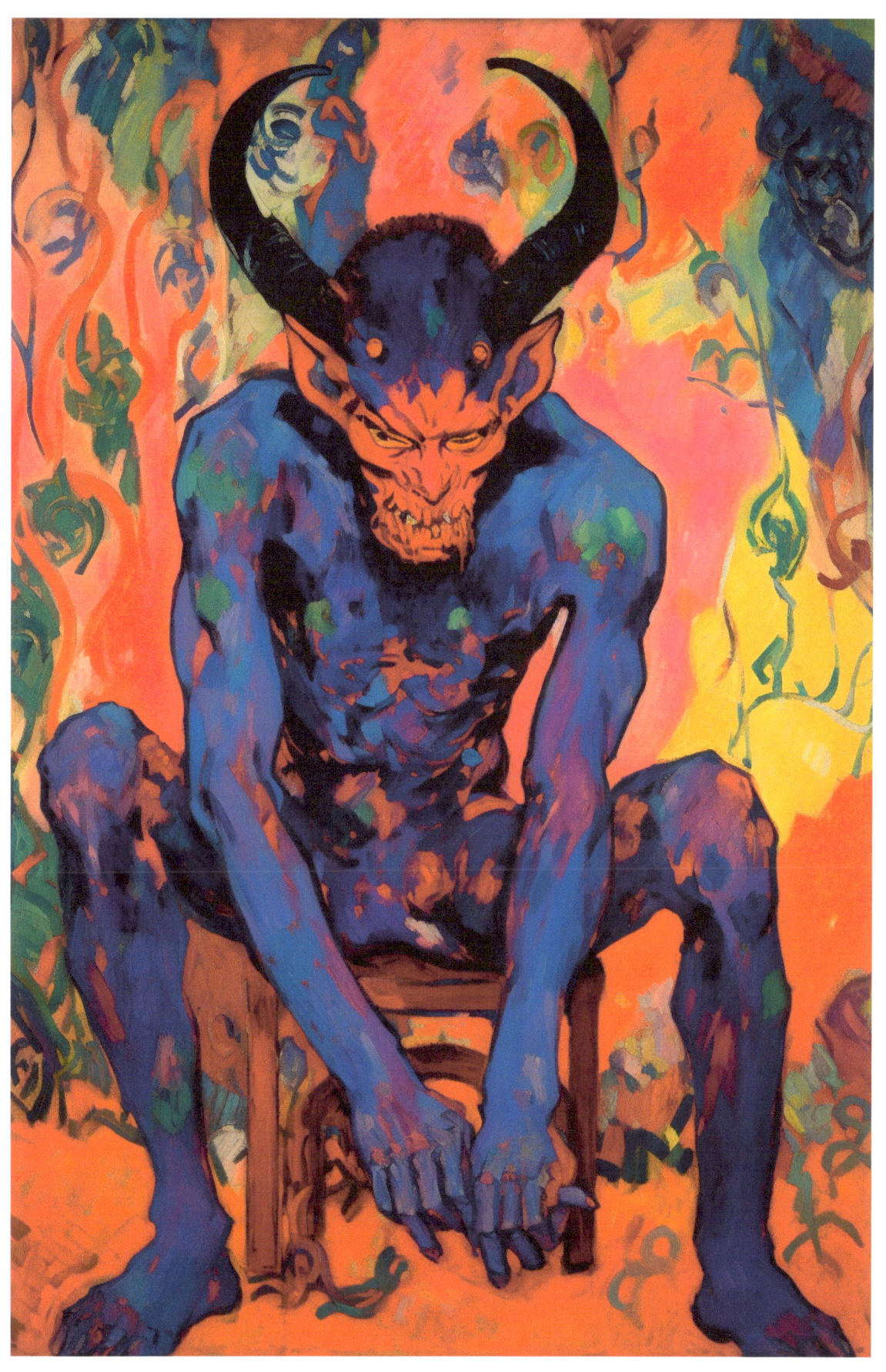

Phantom Limelight

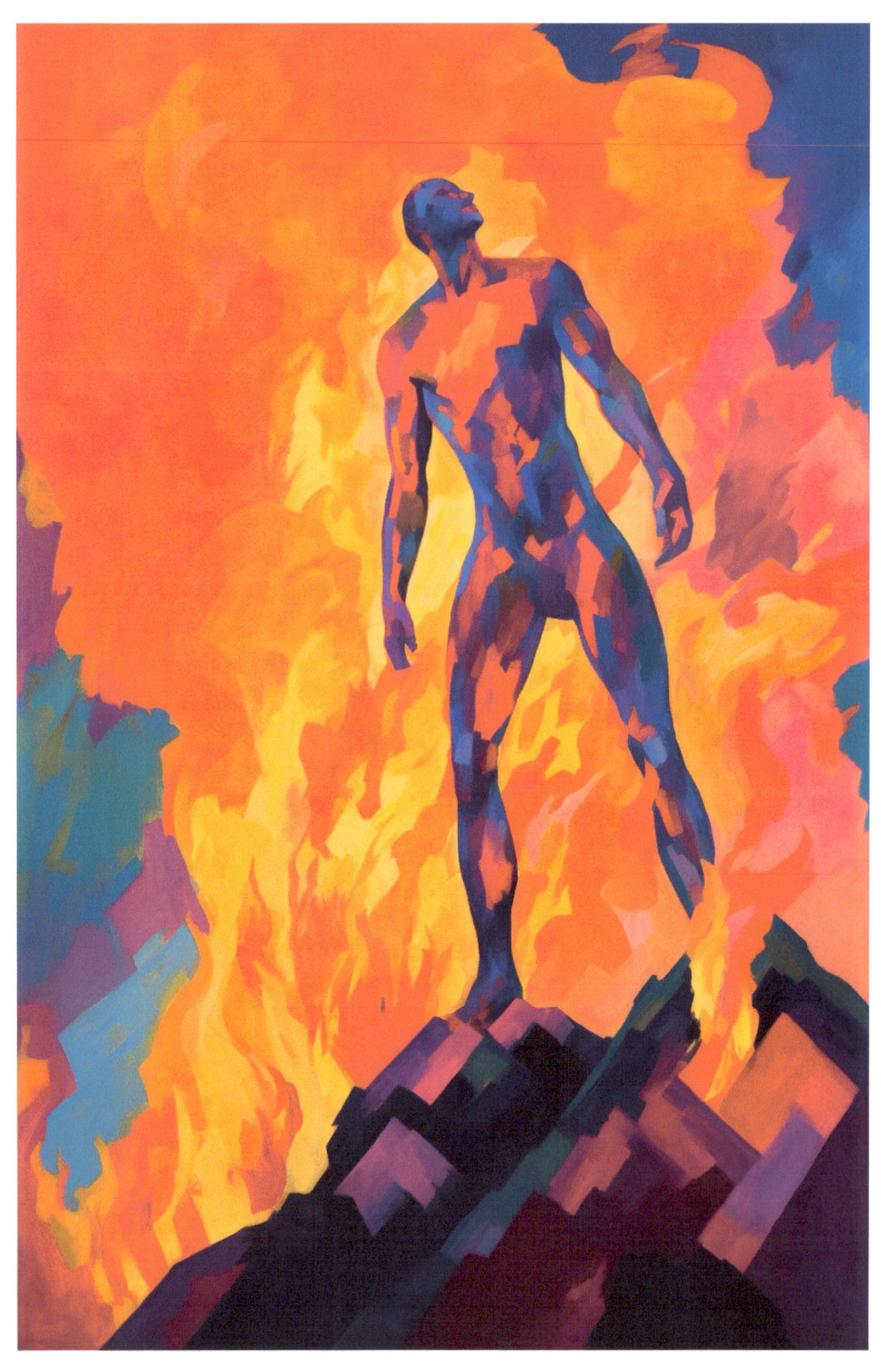

Crimson Carnage

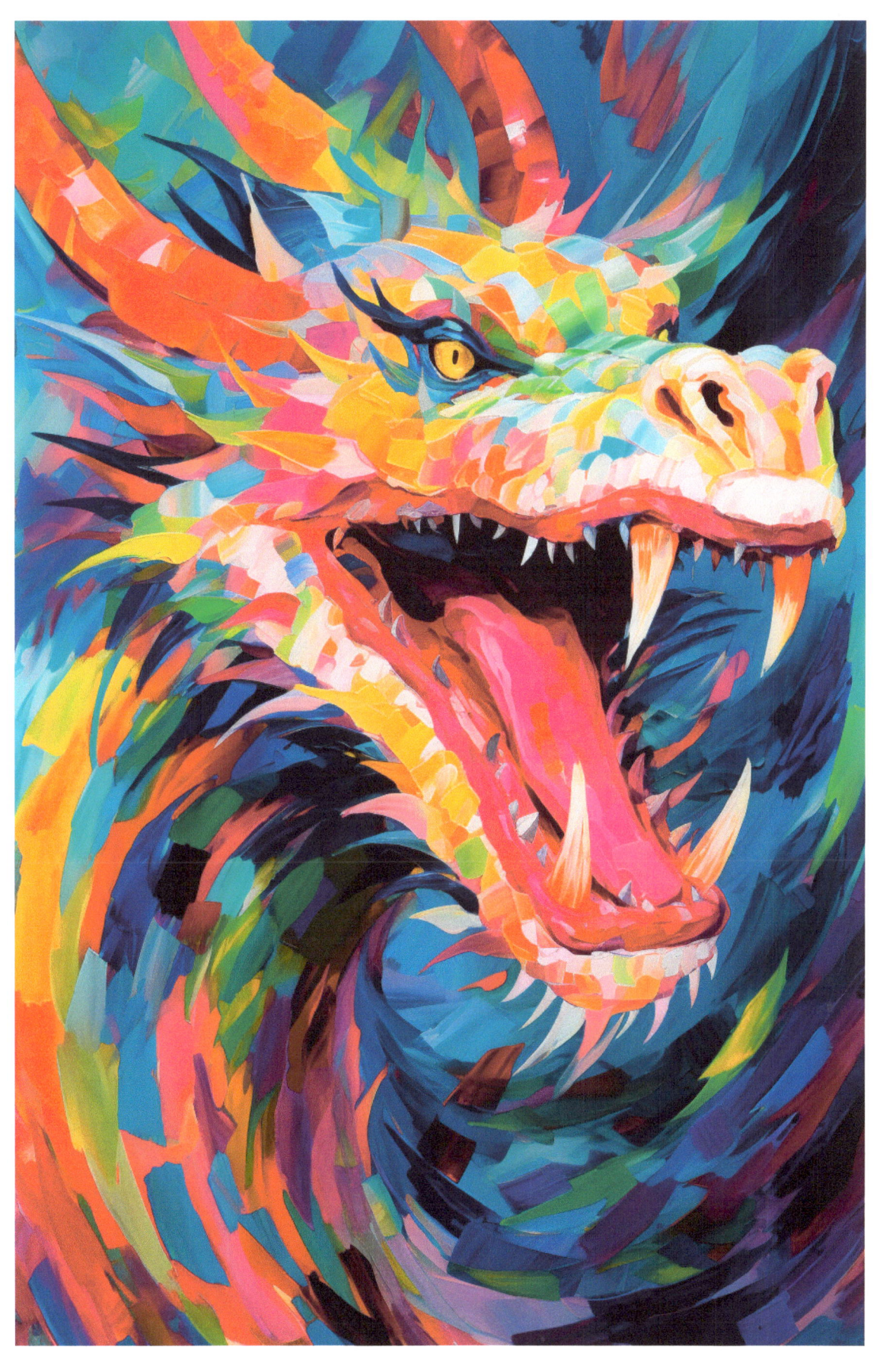

Eruption of Shadows

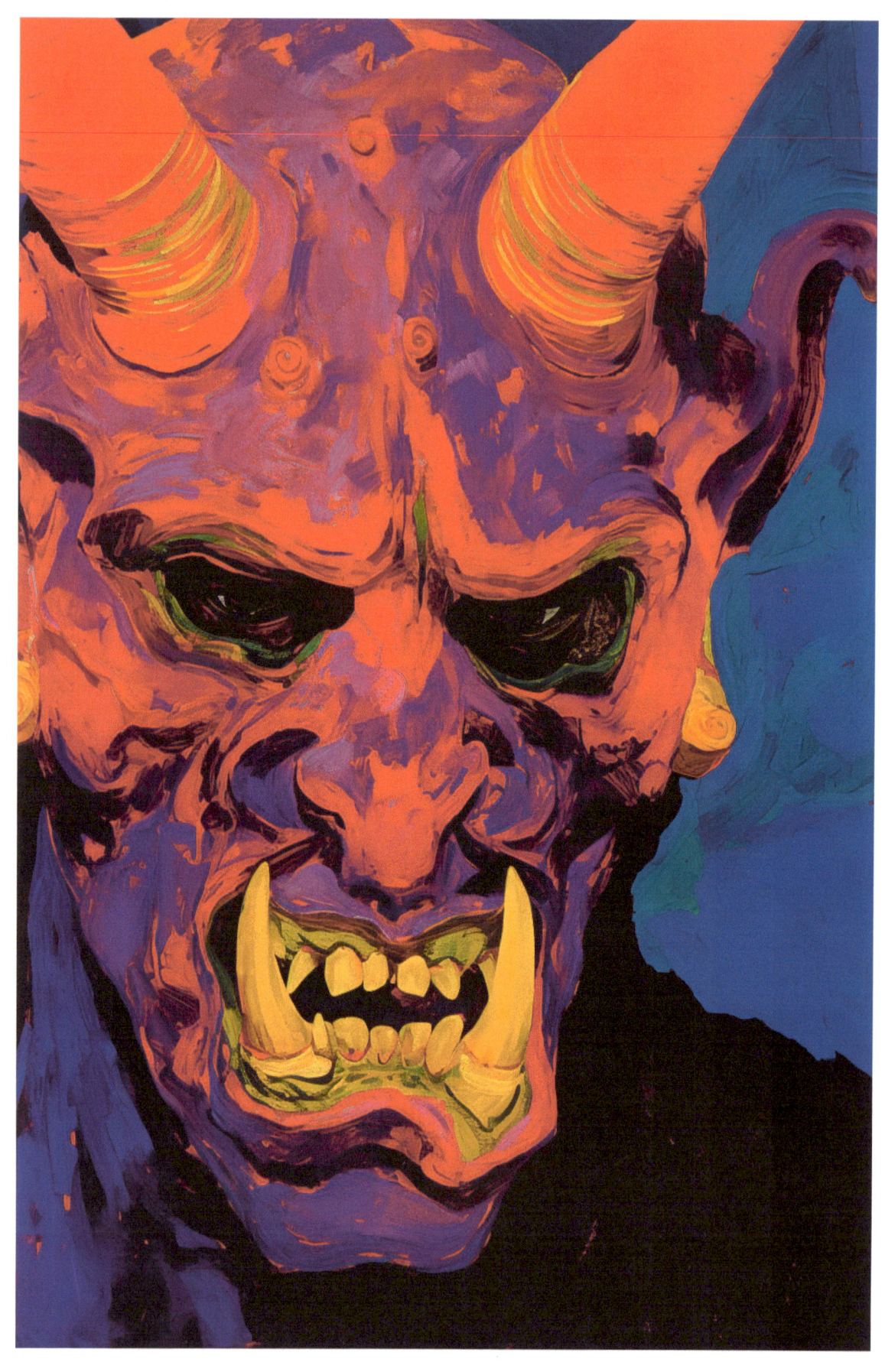

Maelstrom of Malevolence

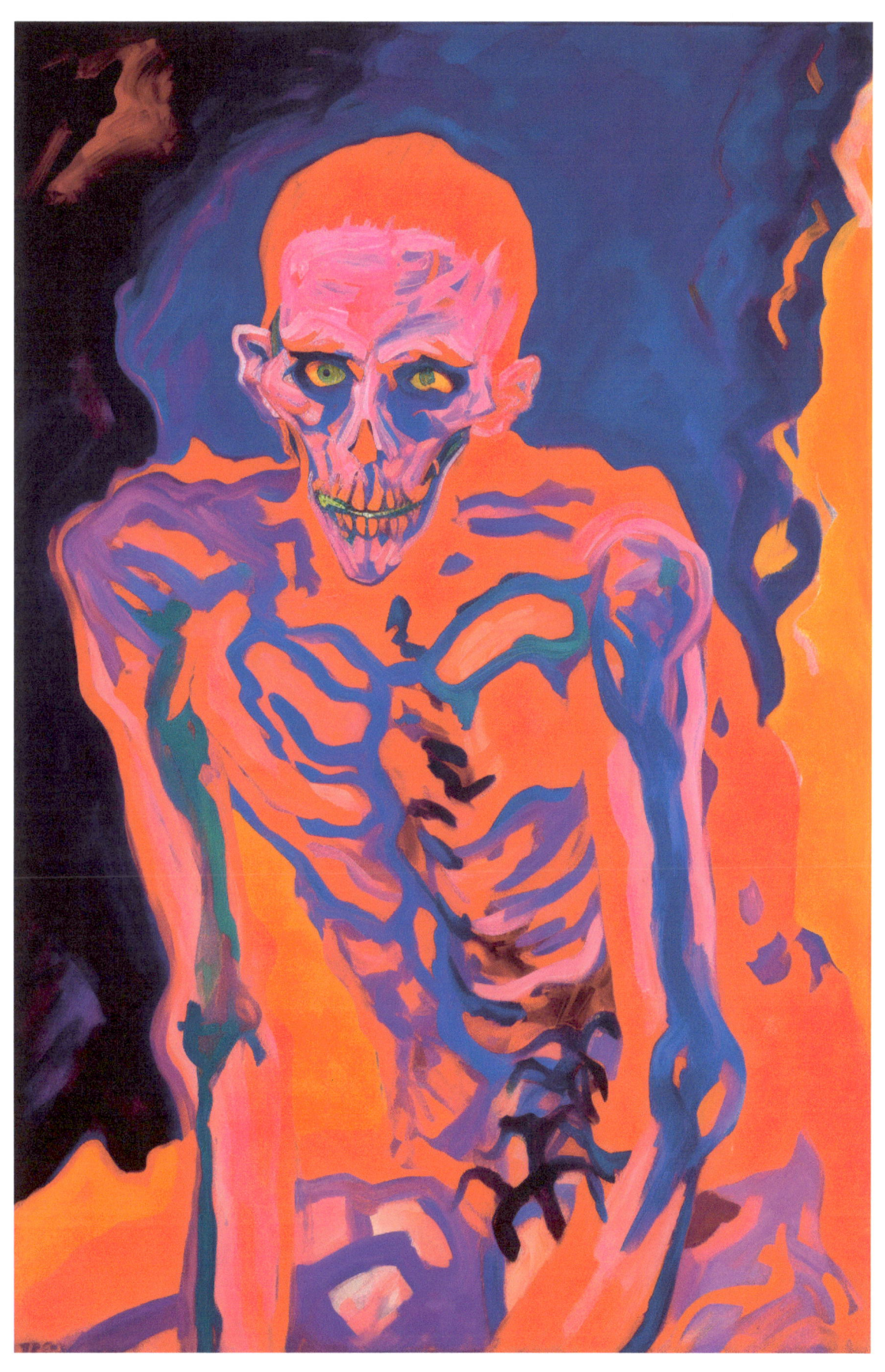

Riot of Ruin

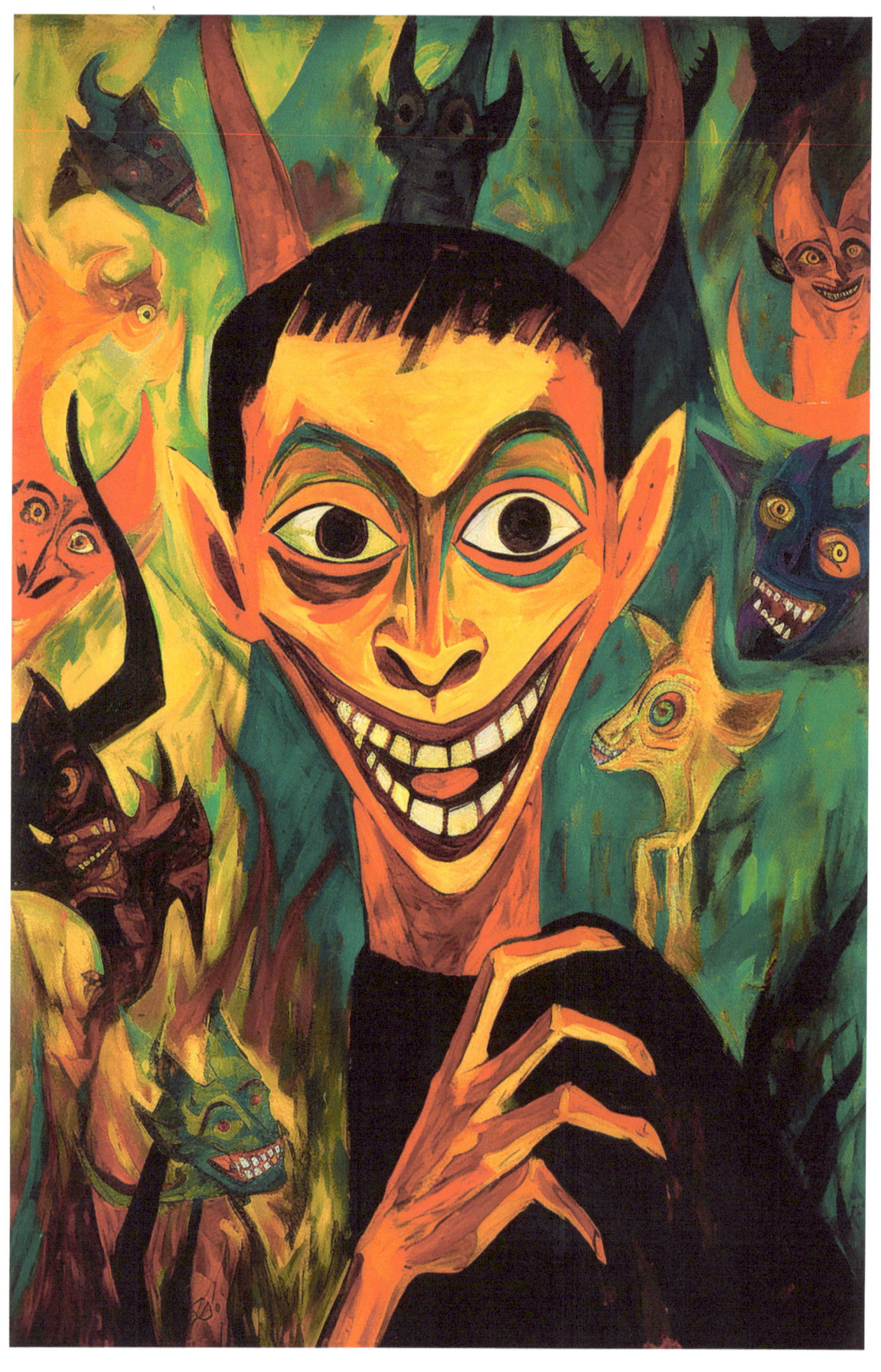

Turbulence of Terror

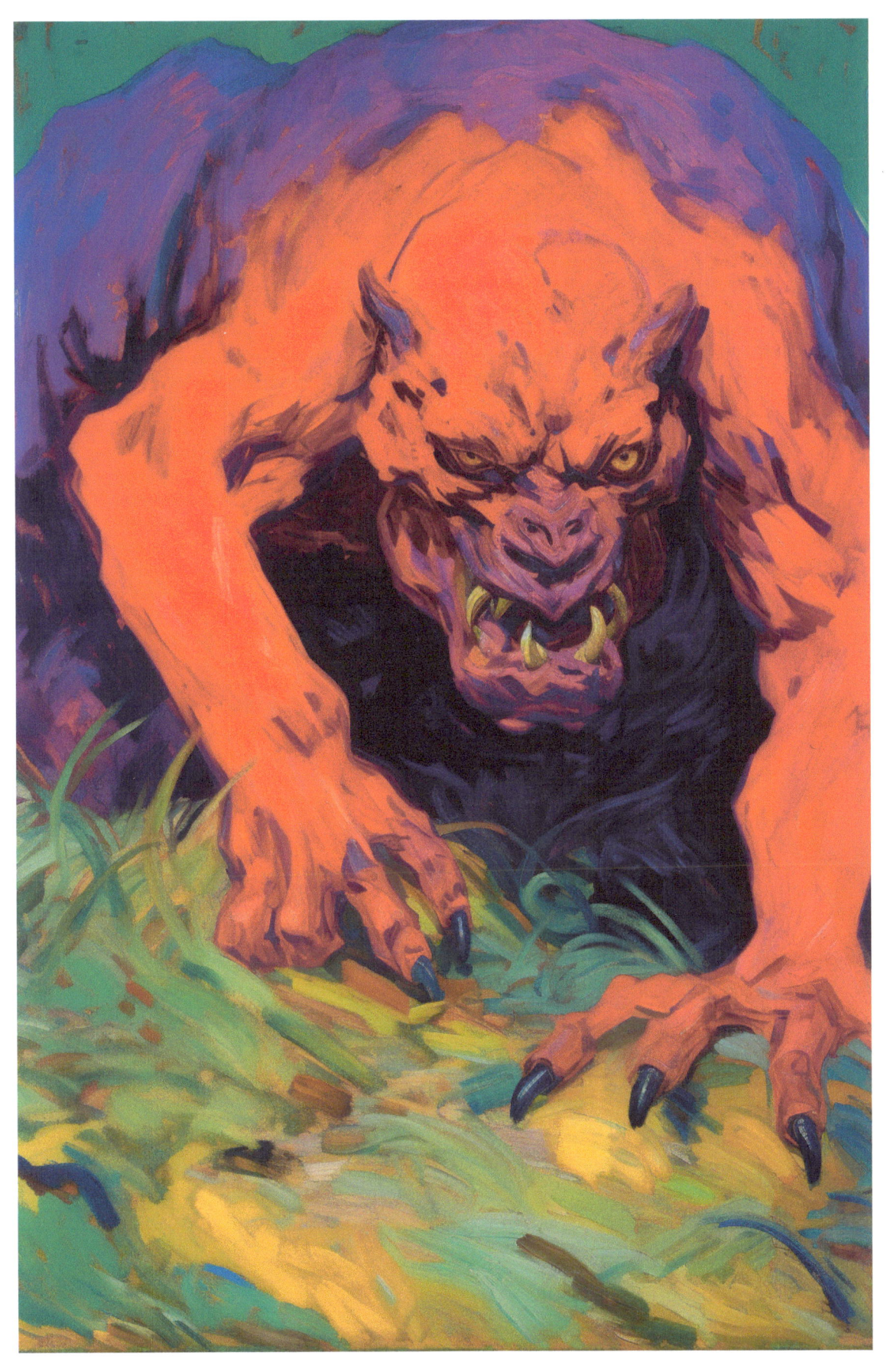

Tempest of Torment

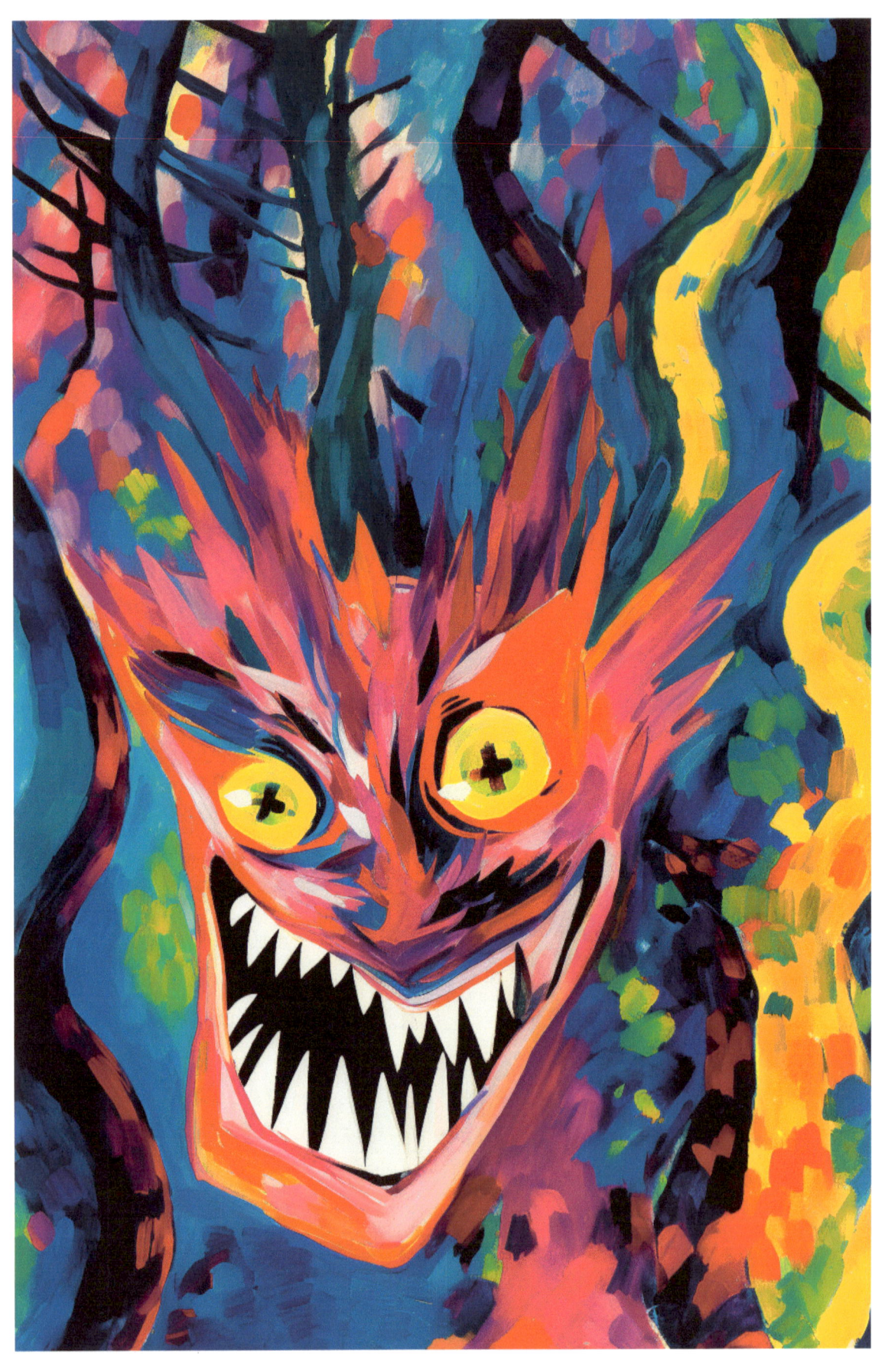

Tempest of Torment

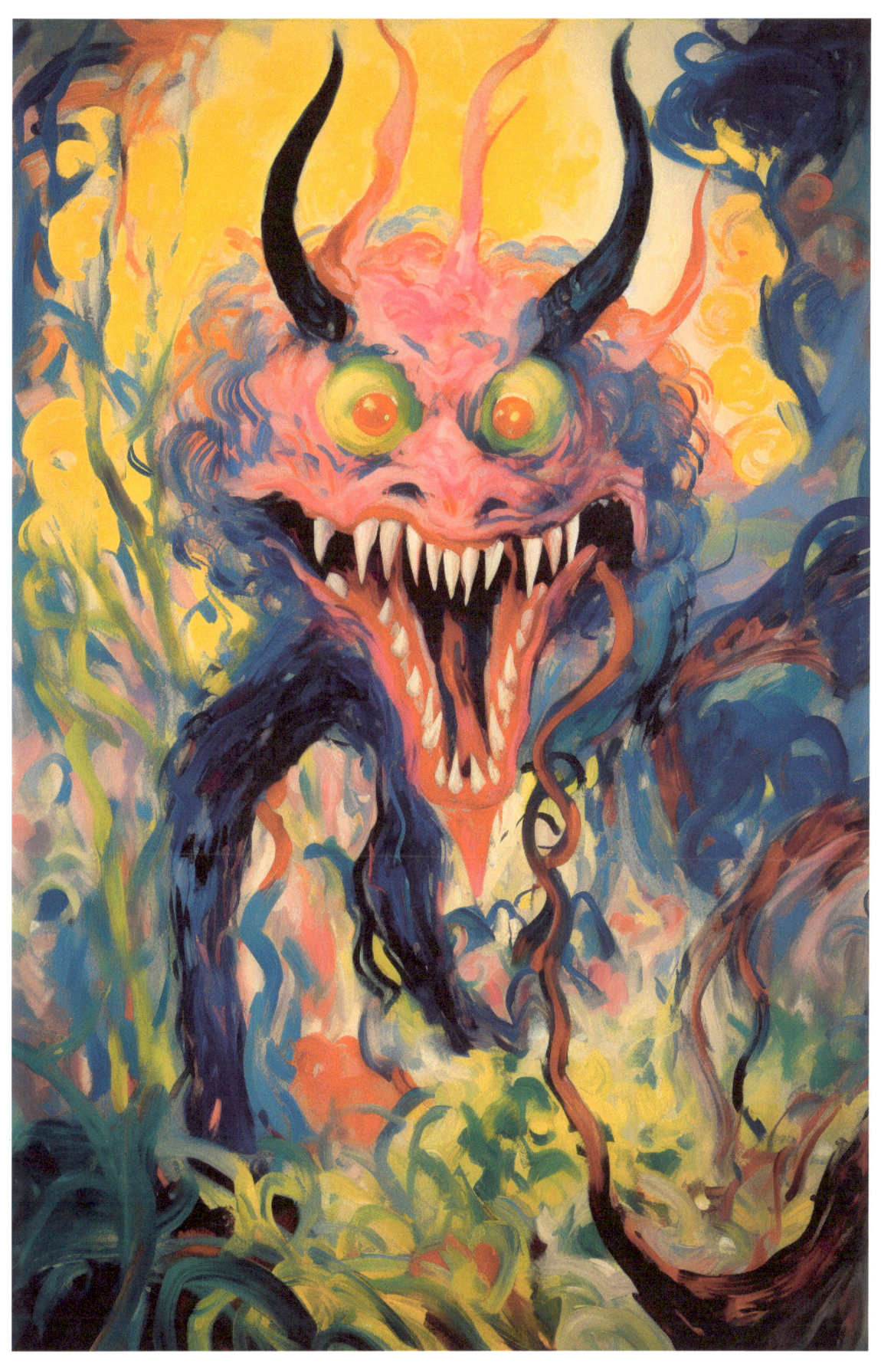

Whirlwind of Woe

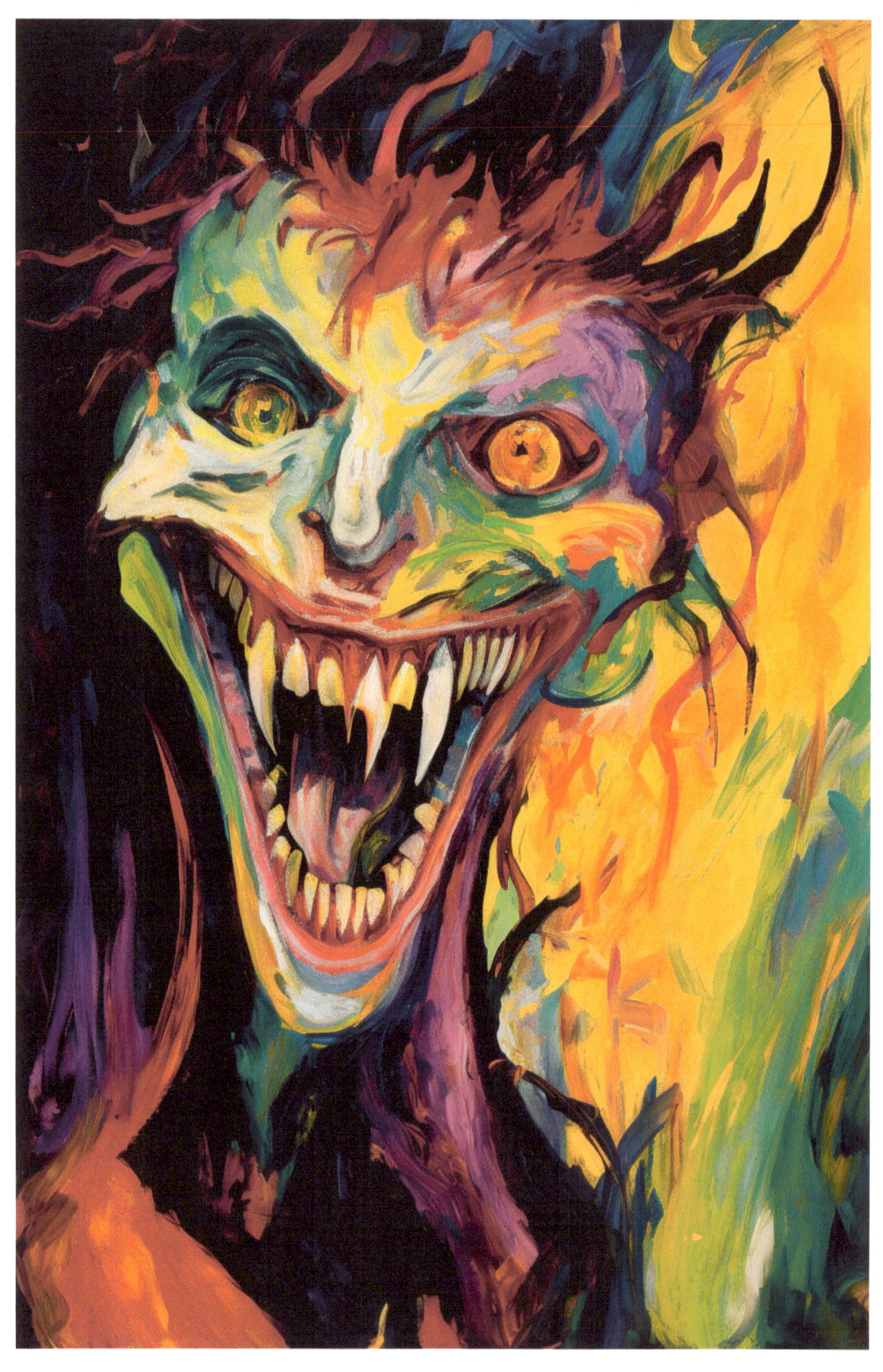

Kaleidoscope of Corpses

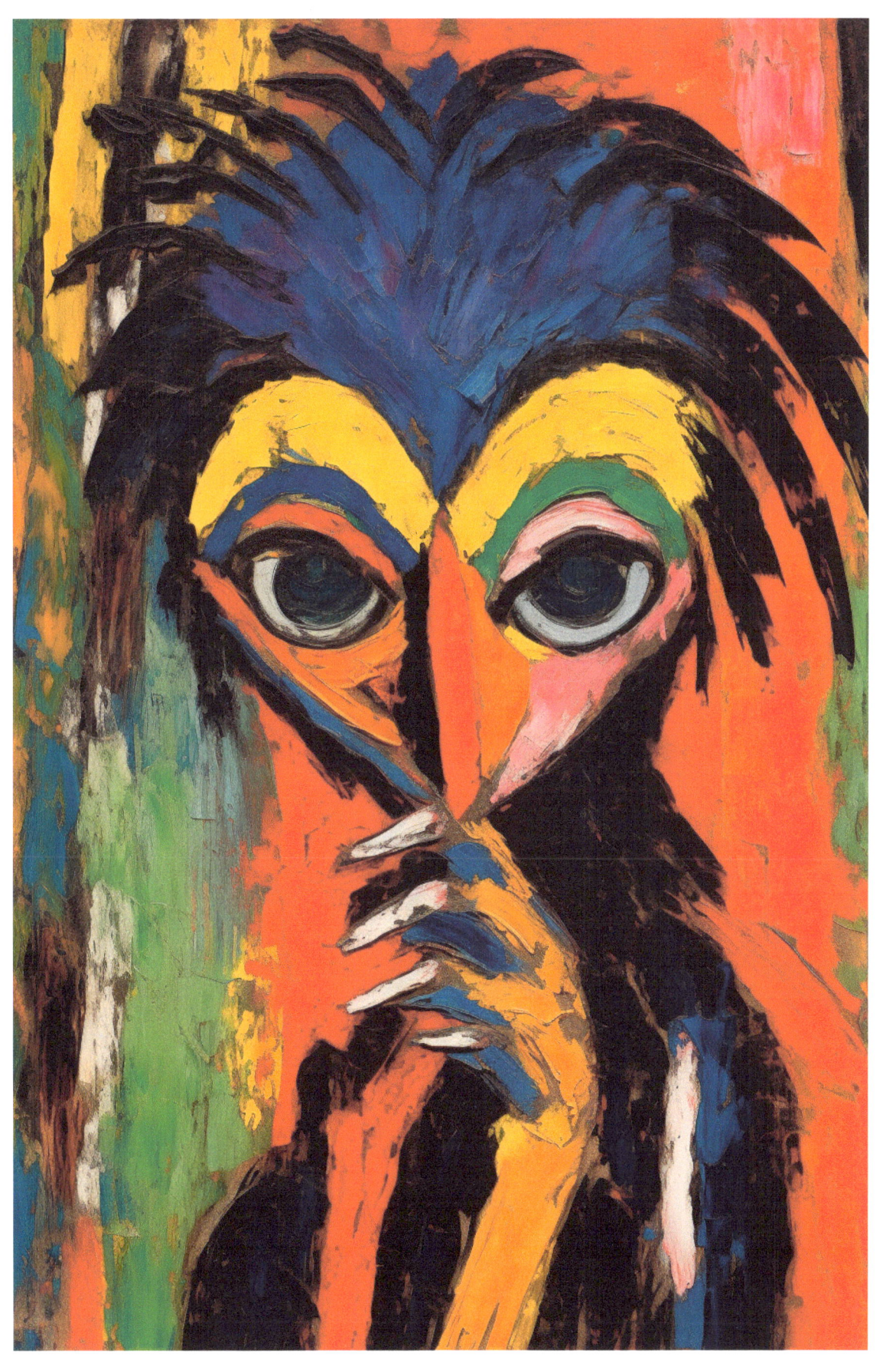

Spectral Storm

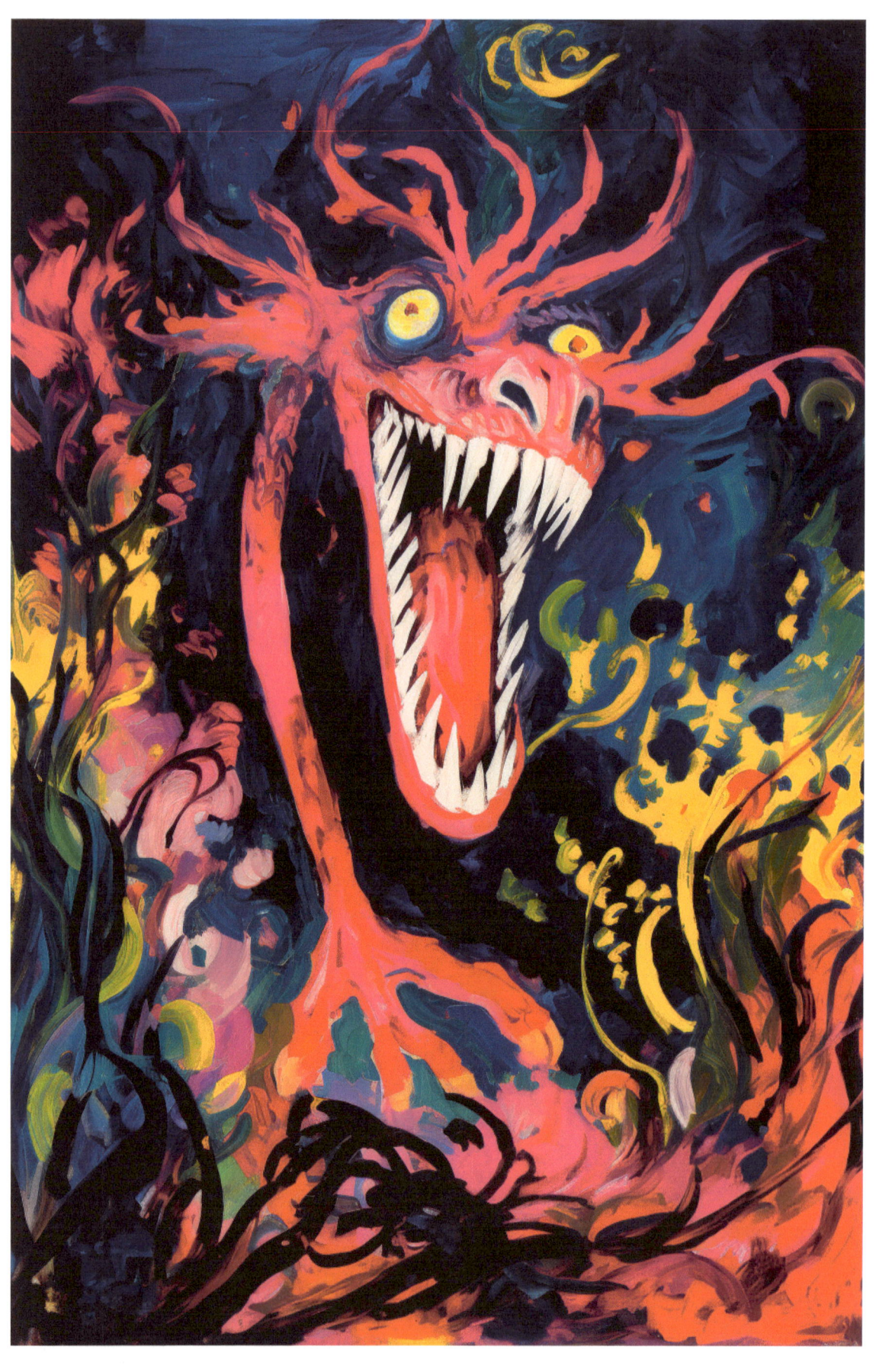

Cacophony of Curses

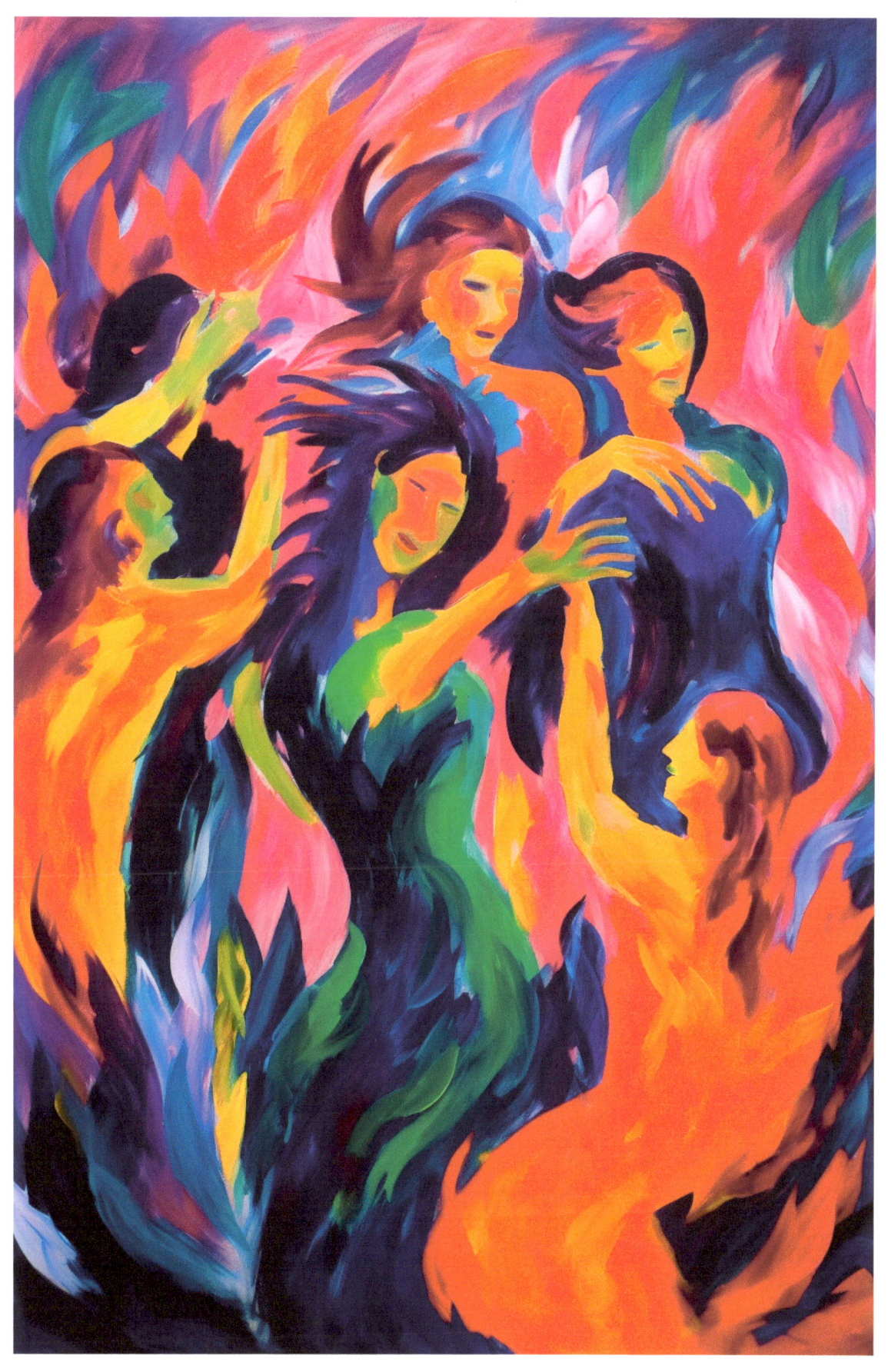

Tempest of Torment

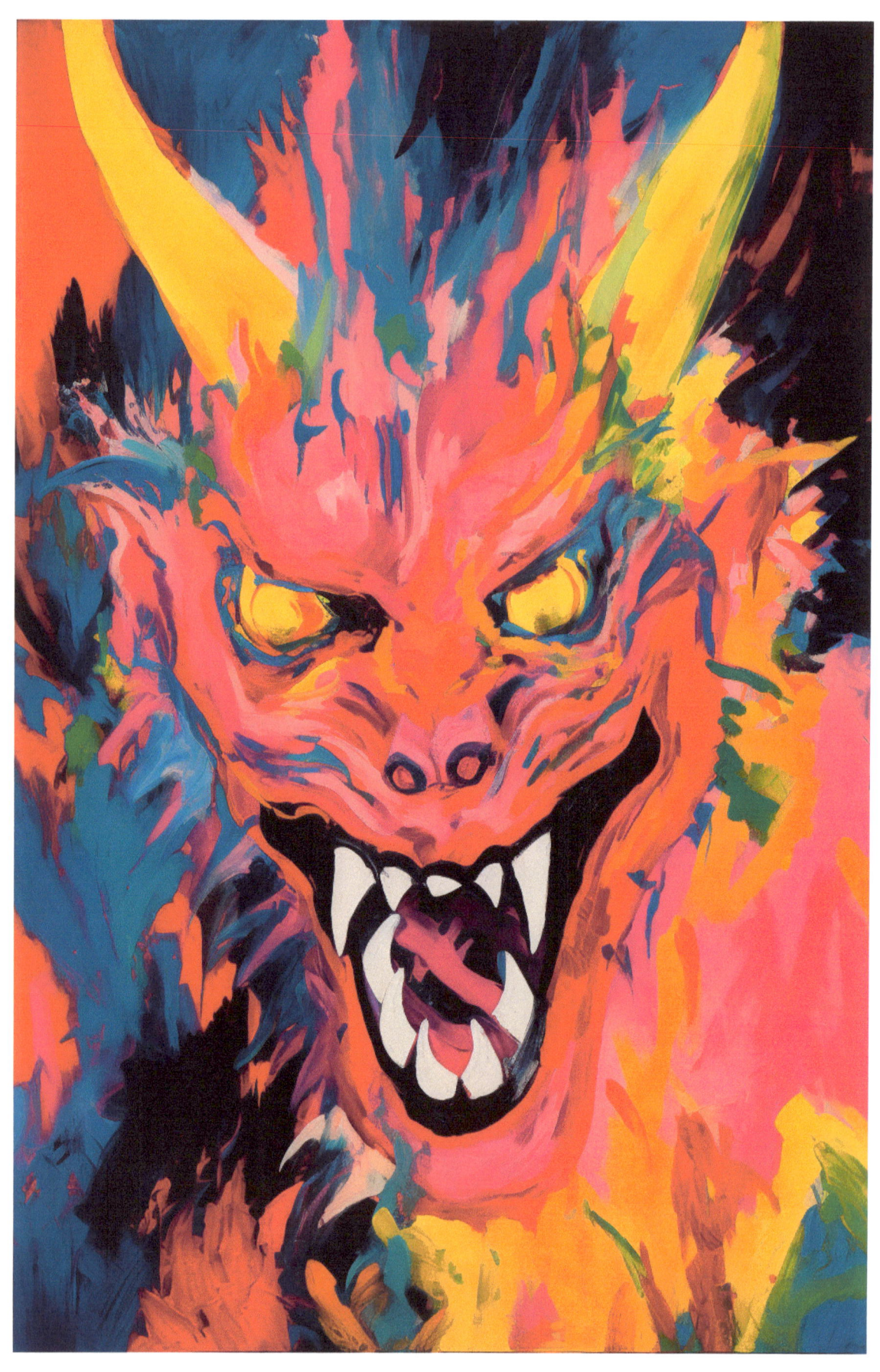

Inferno of Insanity

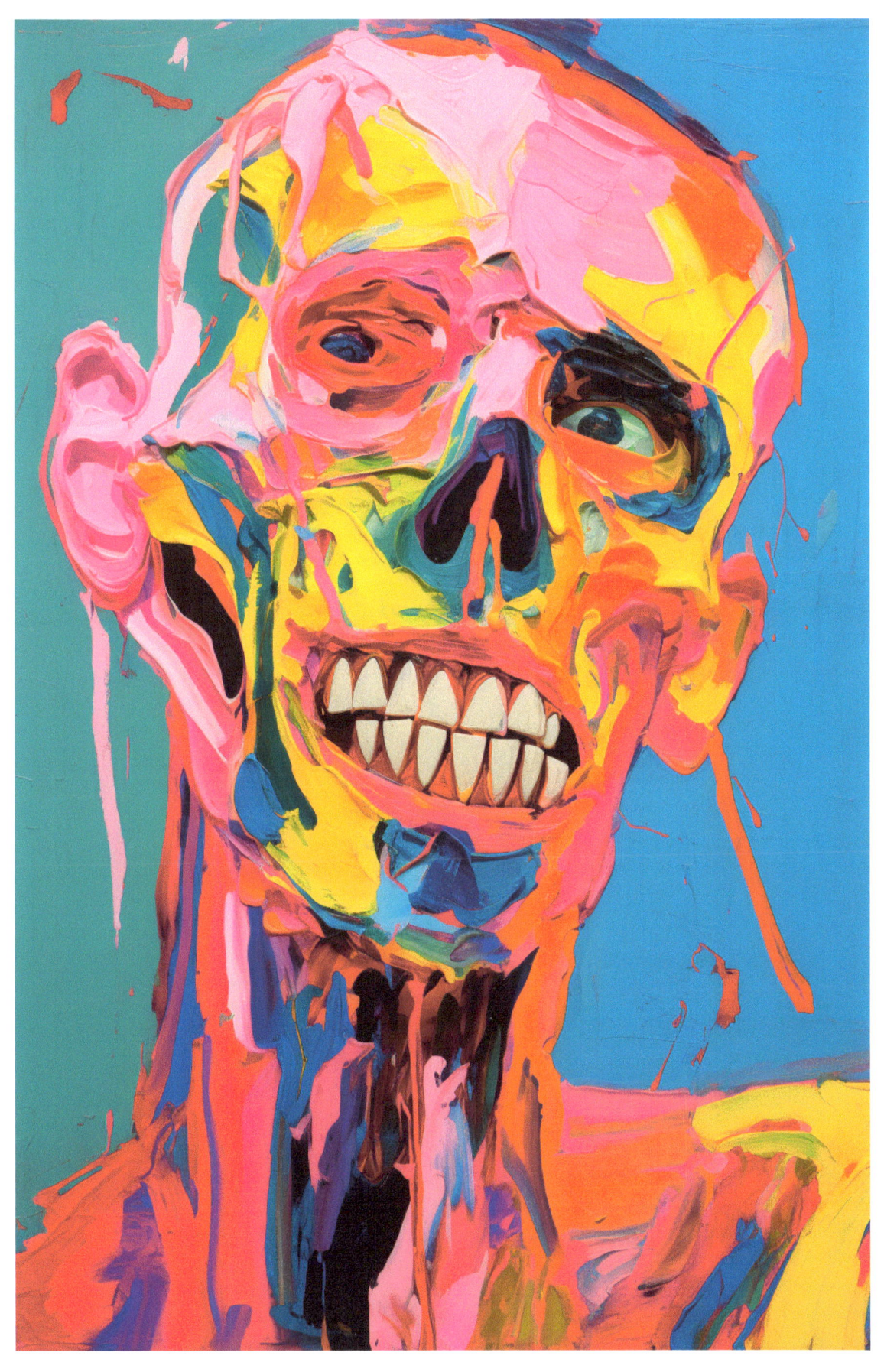

Pandemonium of Phantoms

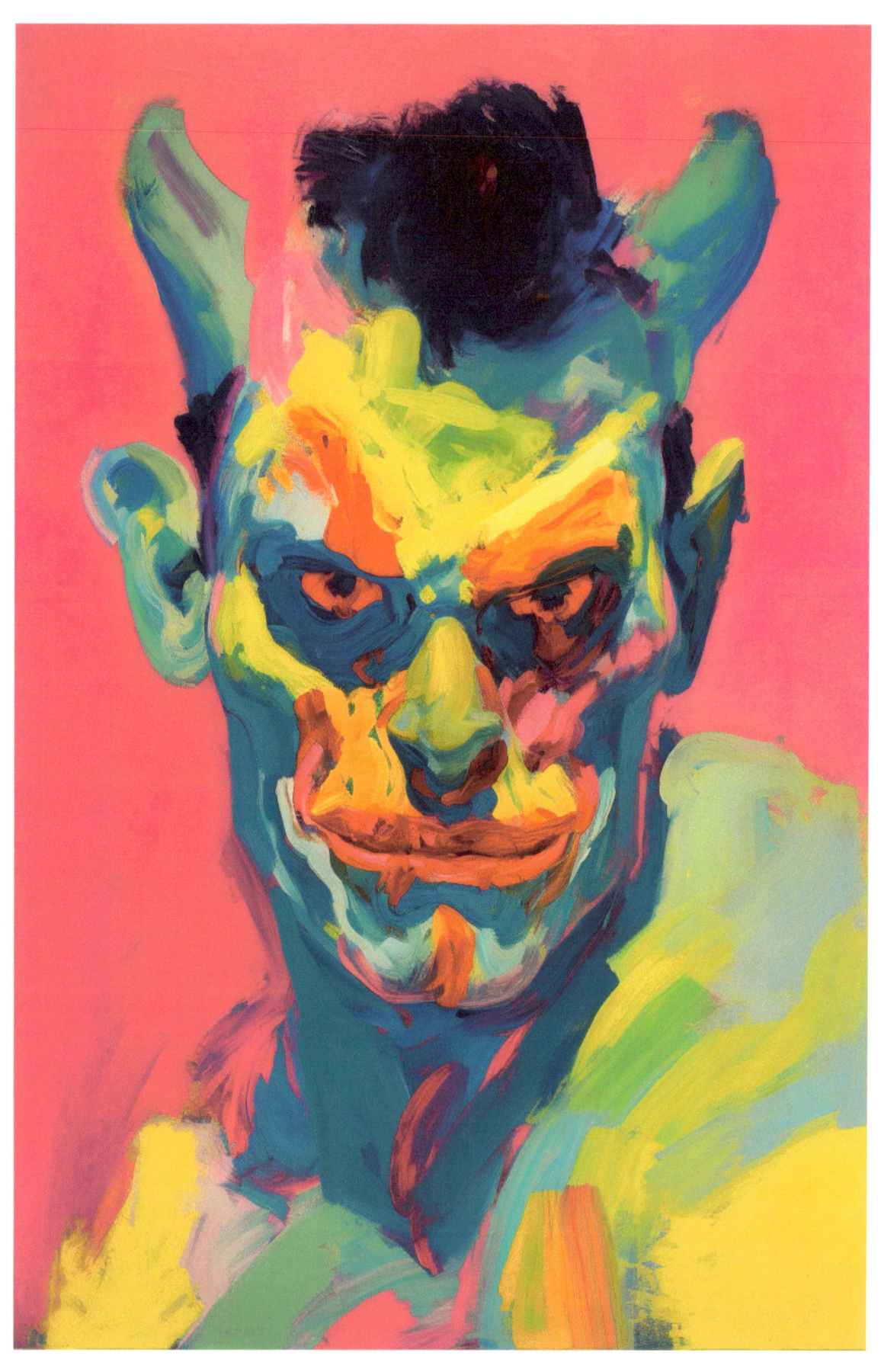

Labyrinth of Lament

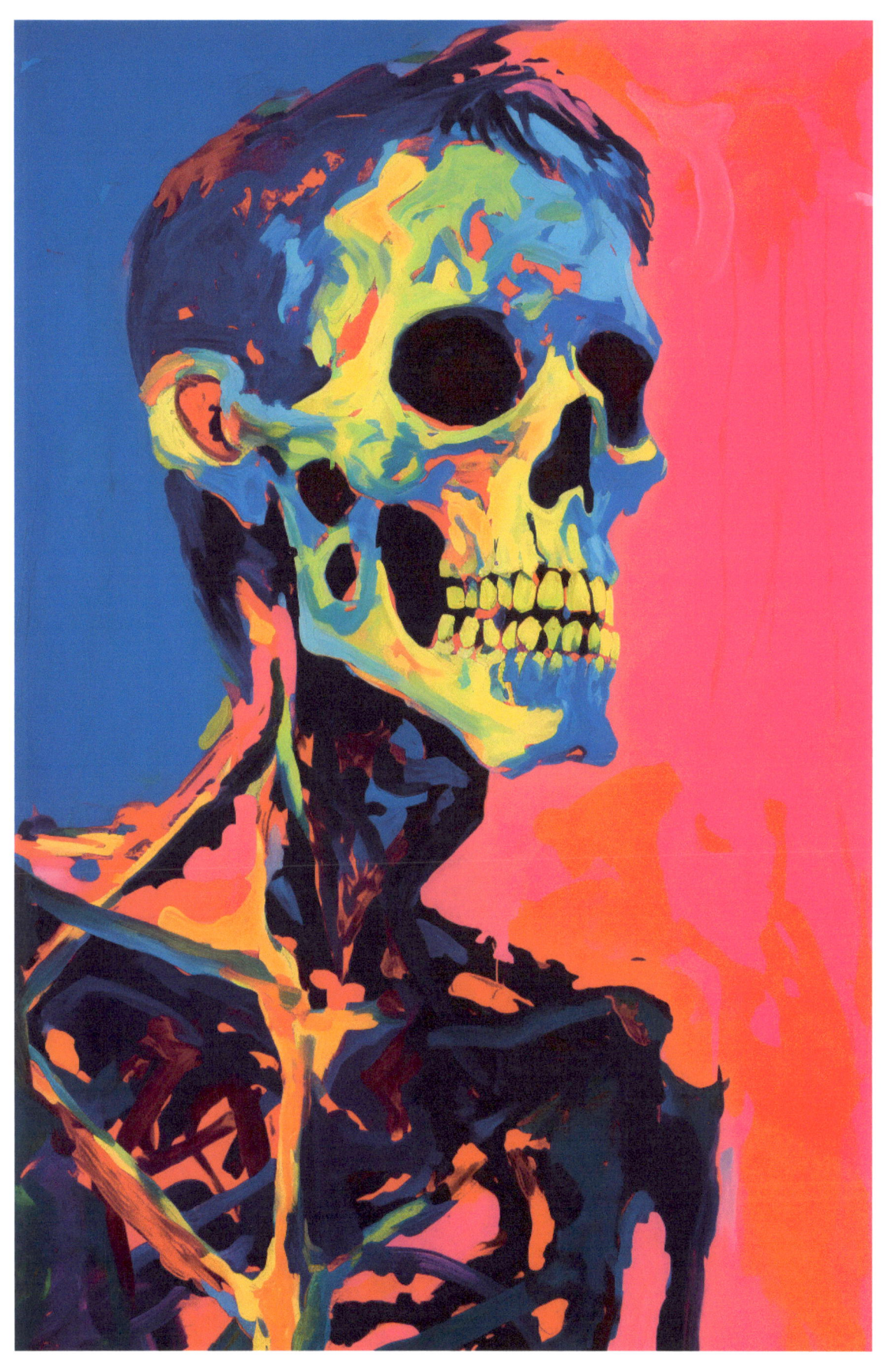

Deluge of Despair

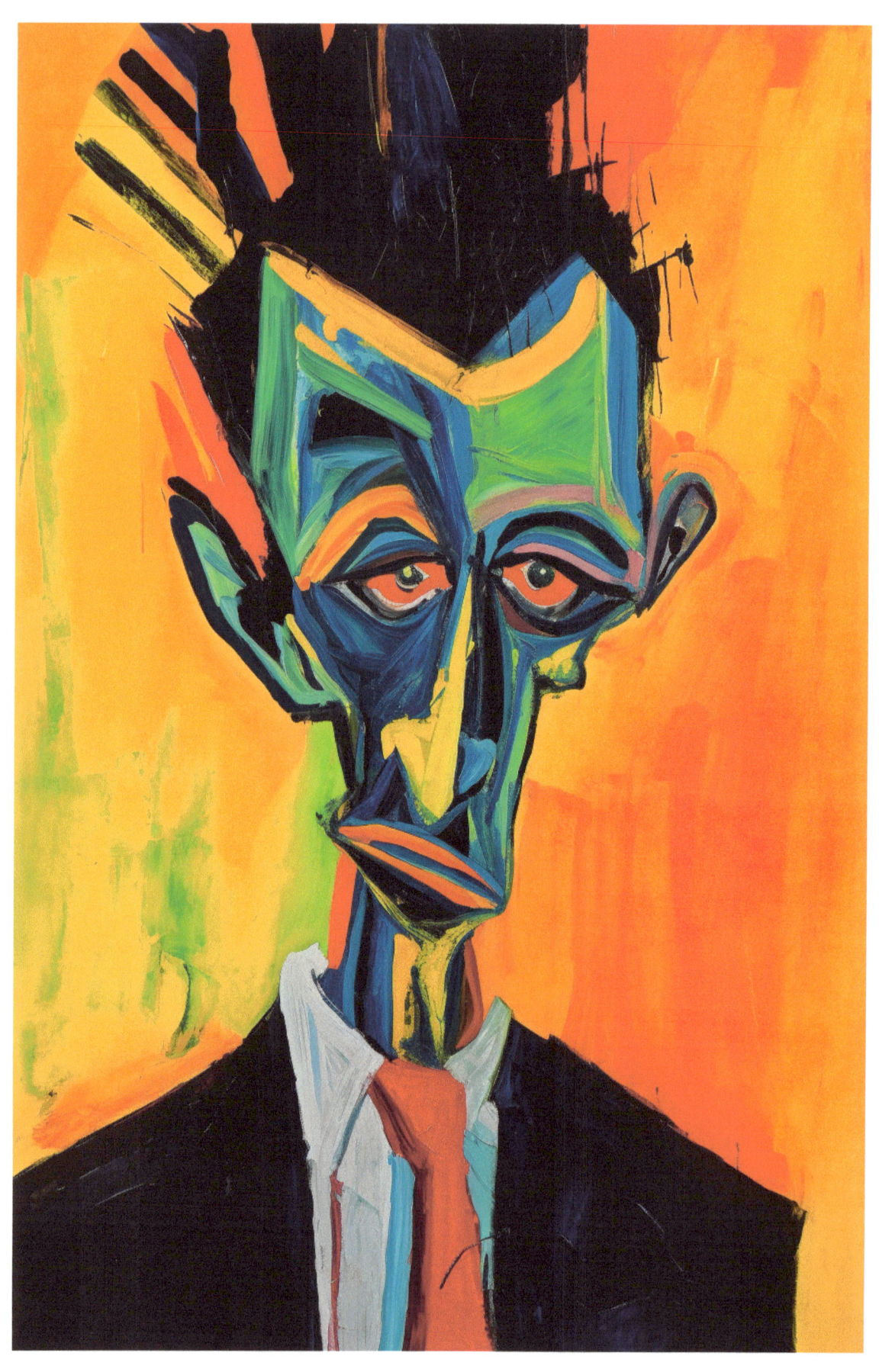

Chromatic Chaos

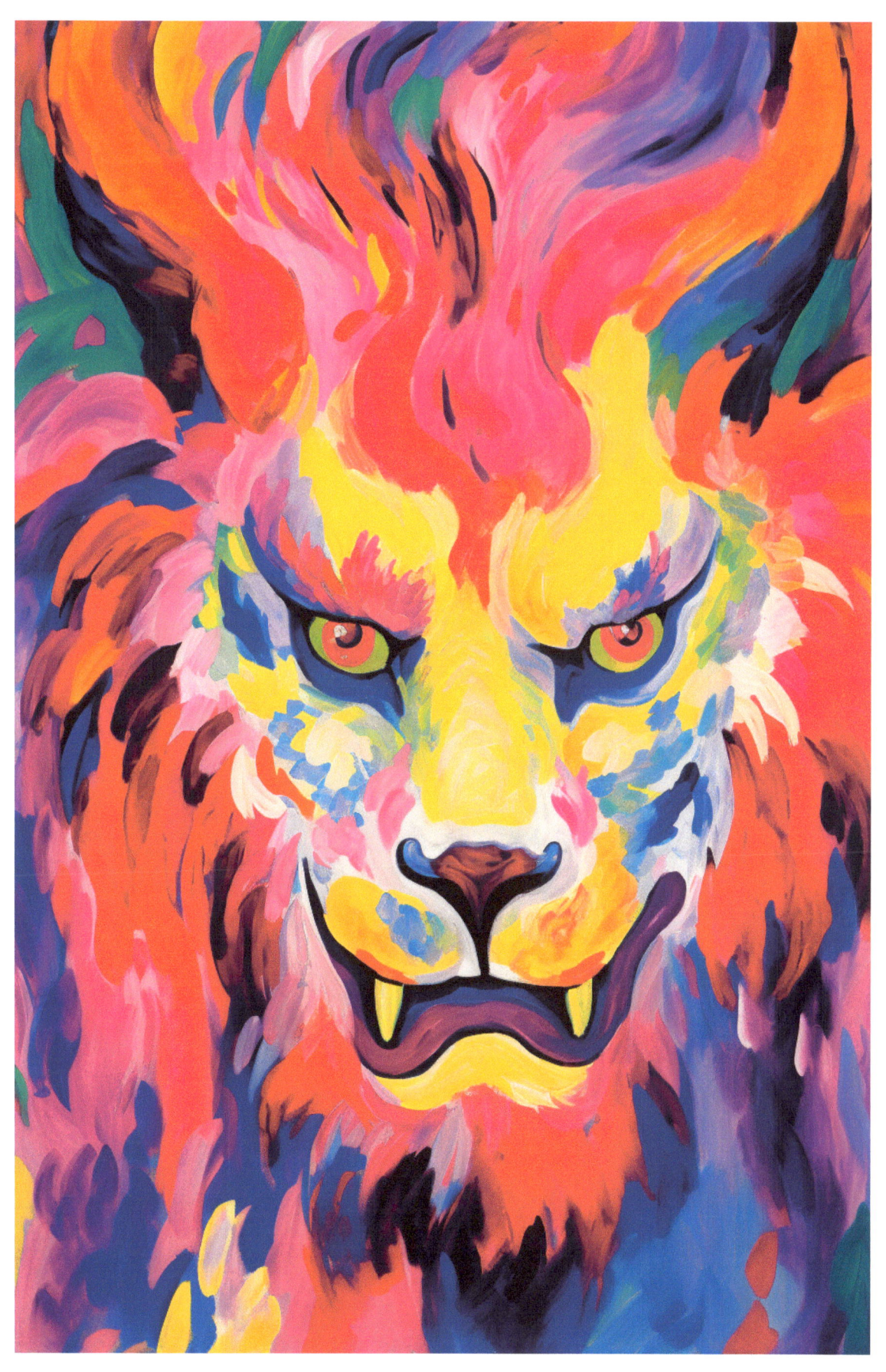

Radiance of Ruination

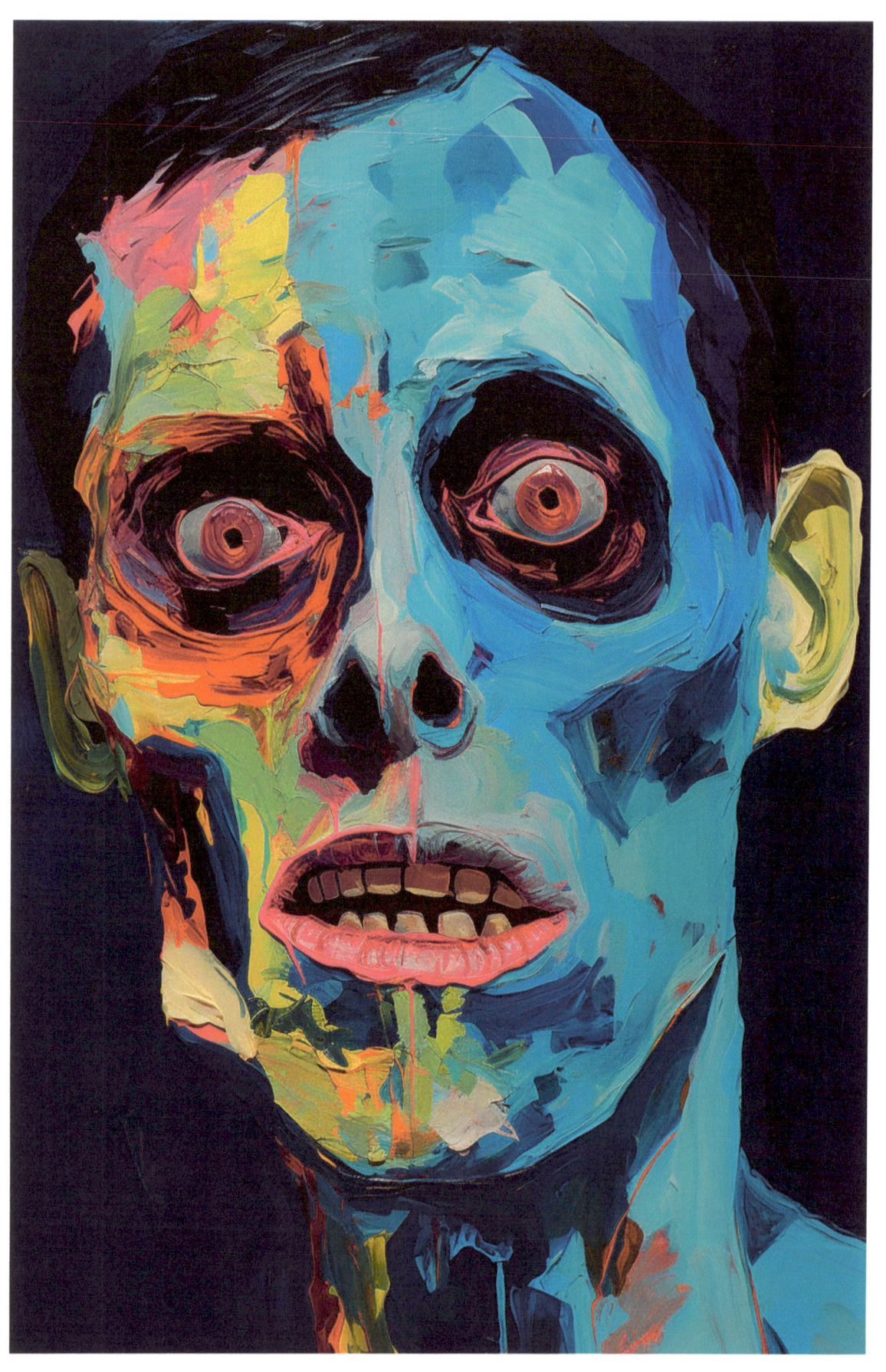

Carnival of Carrion

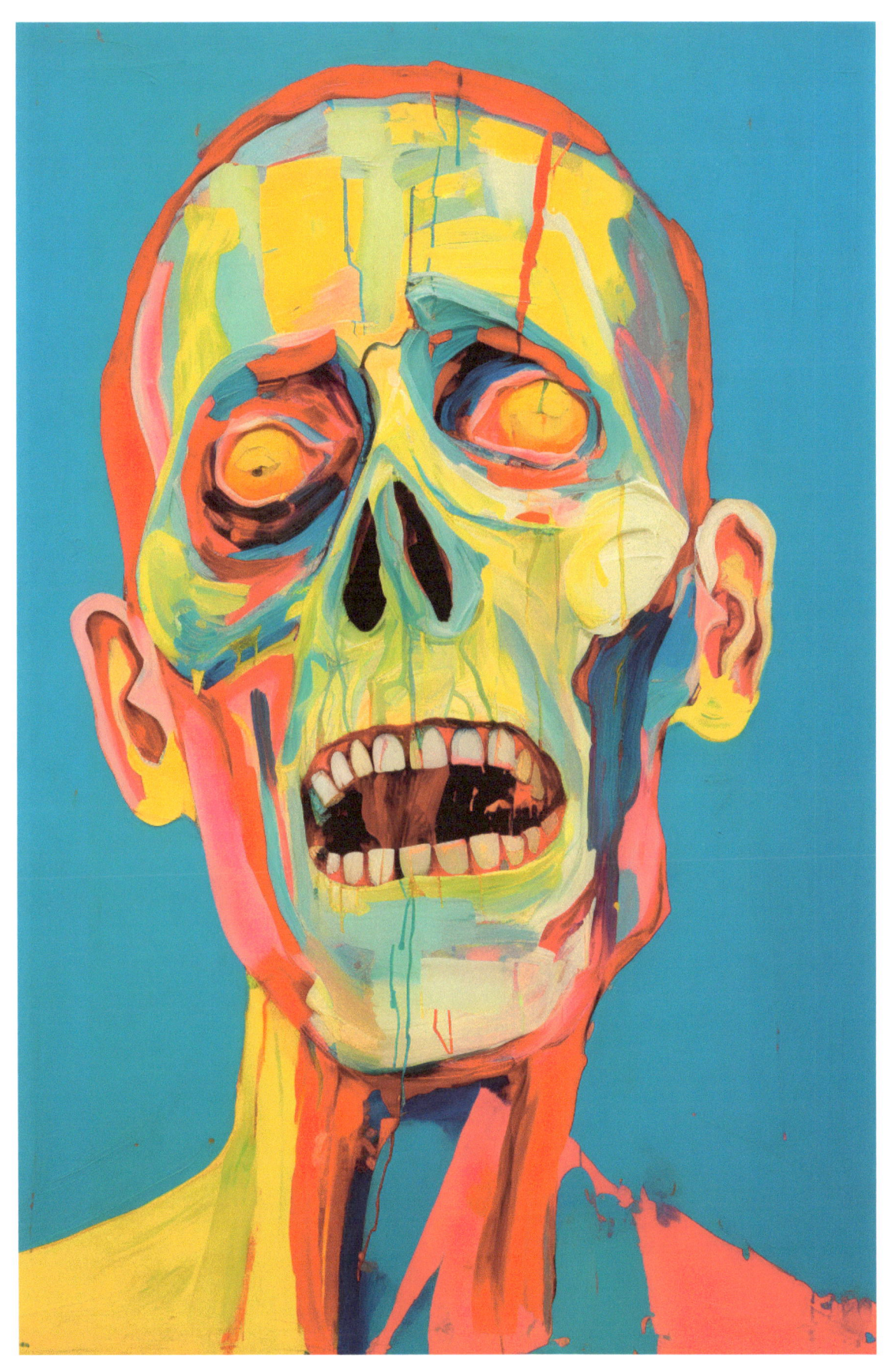

Blaze of Bloodlust

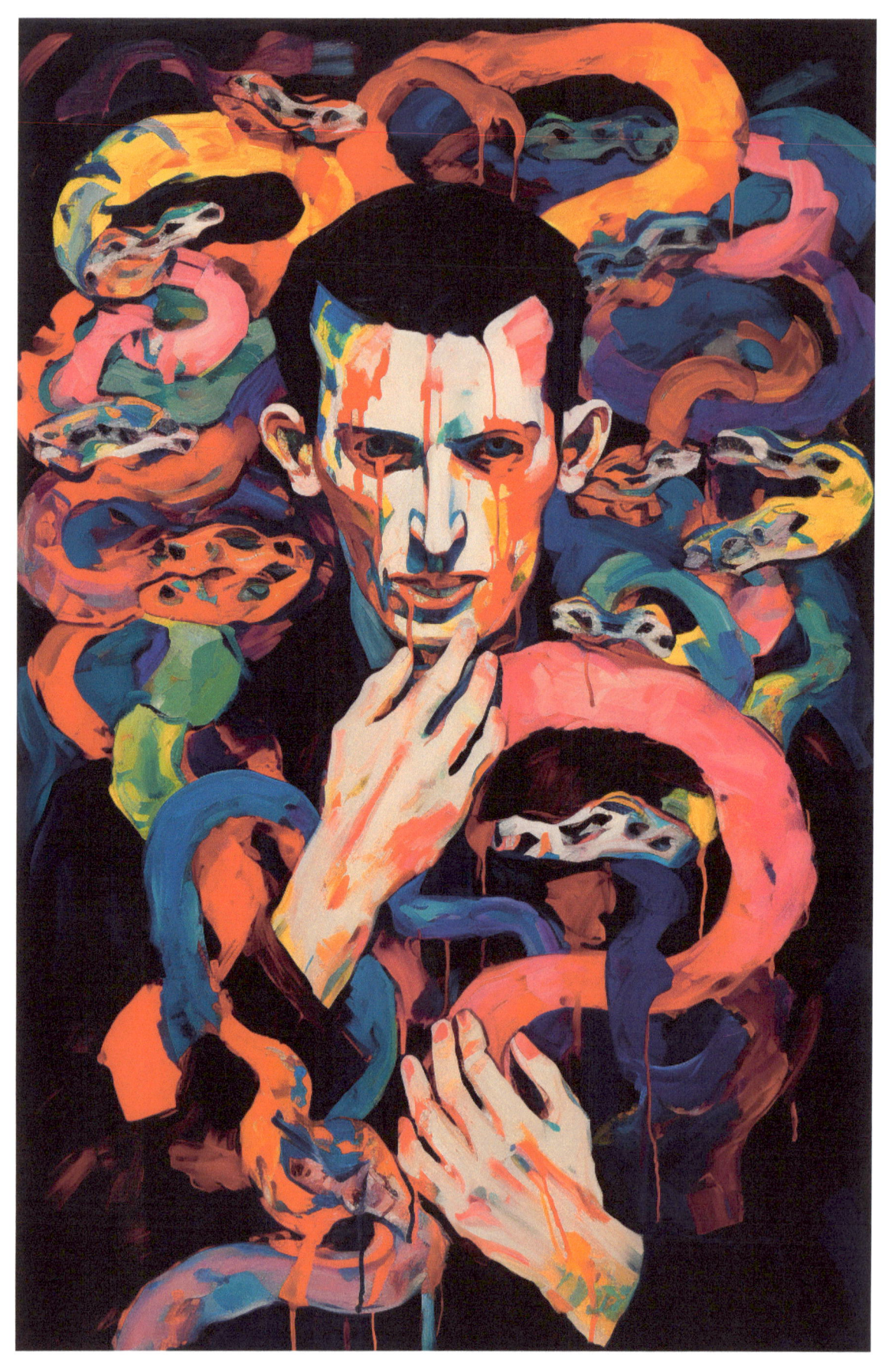

Gale of Ghouls

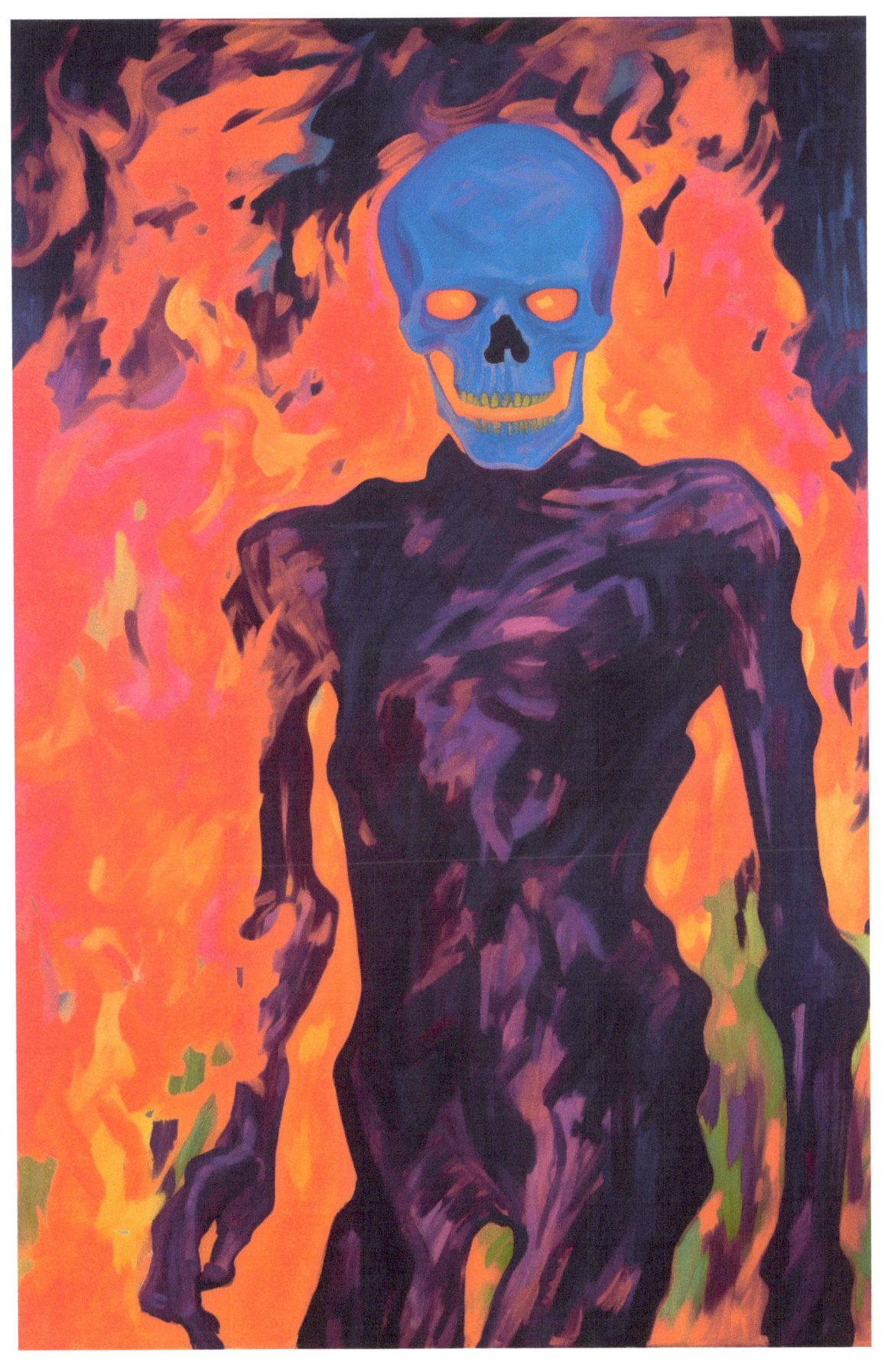

Abyss of Apparitions

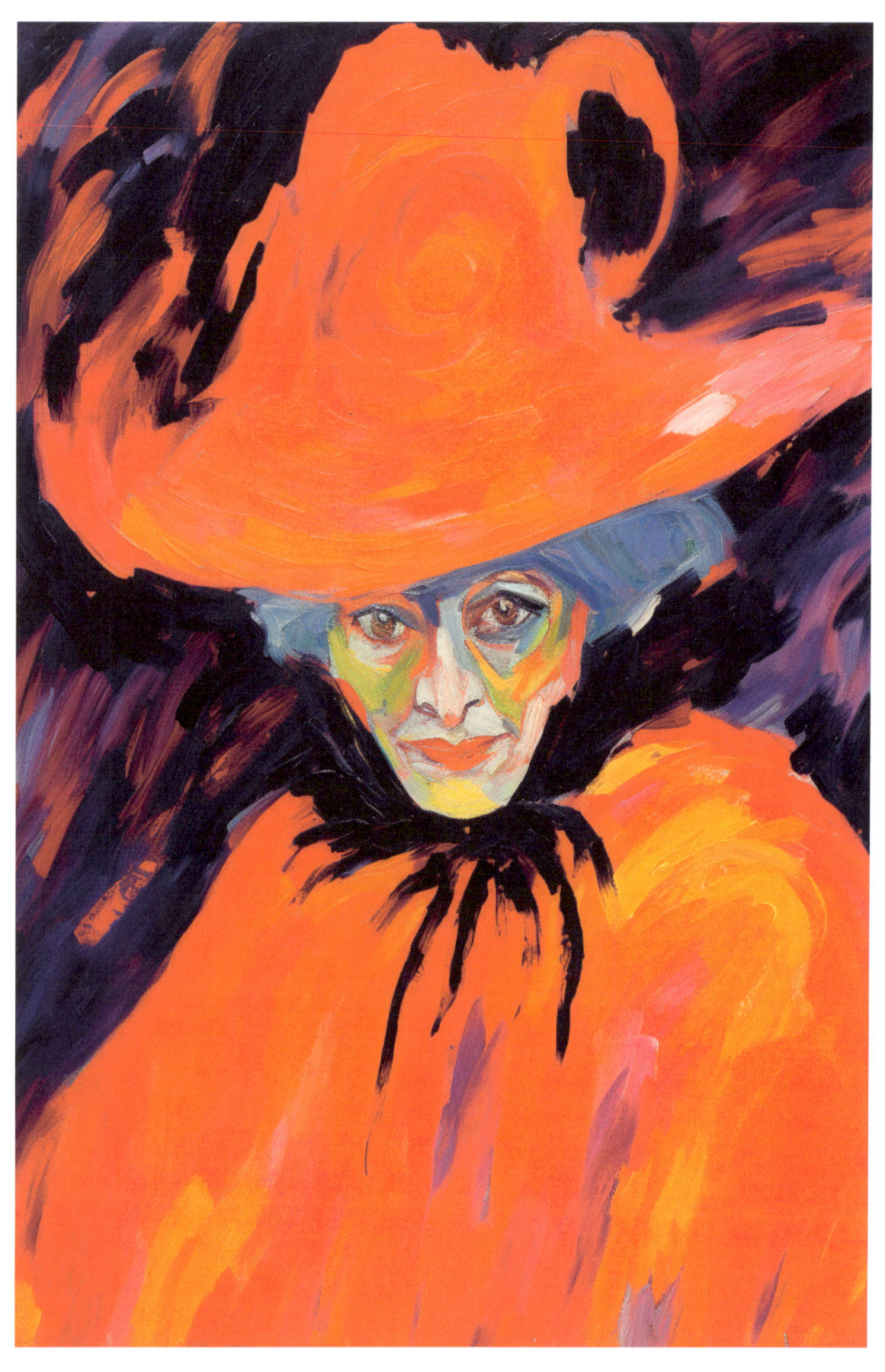

Blitz of Brimstone

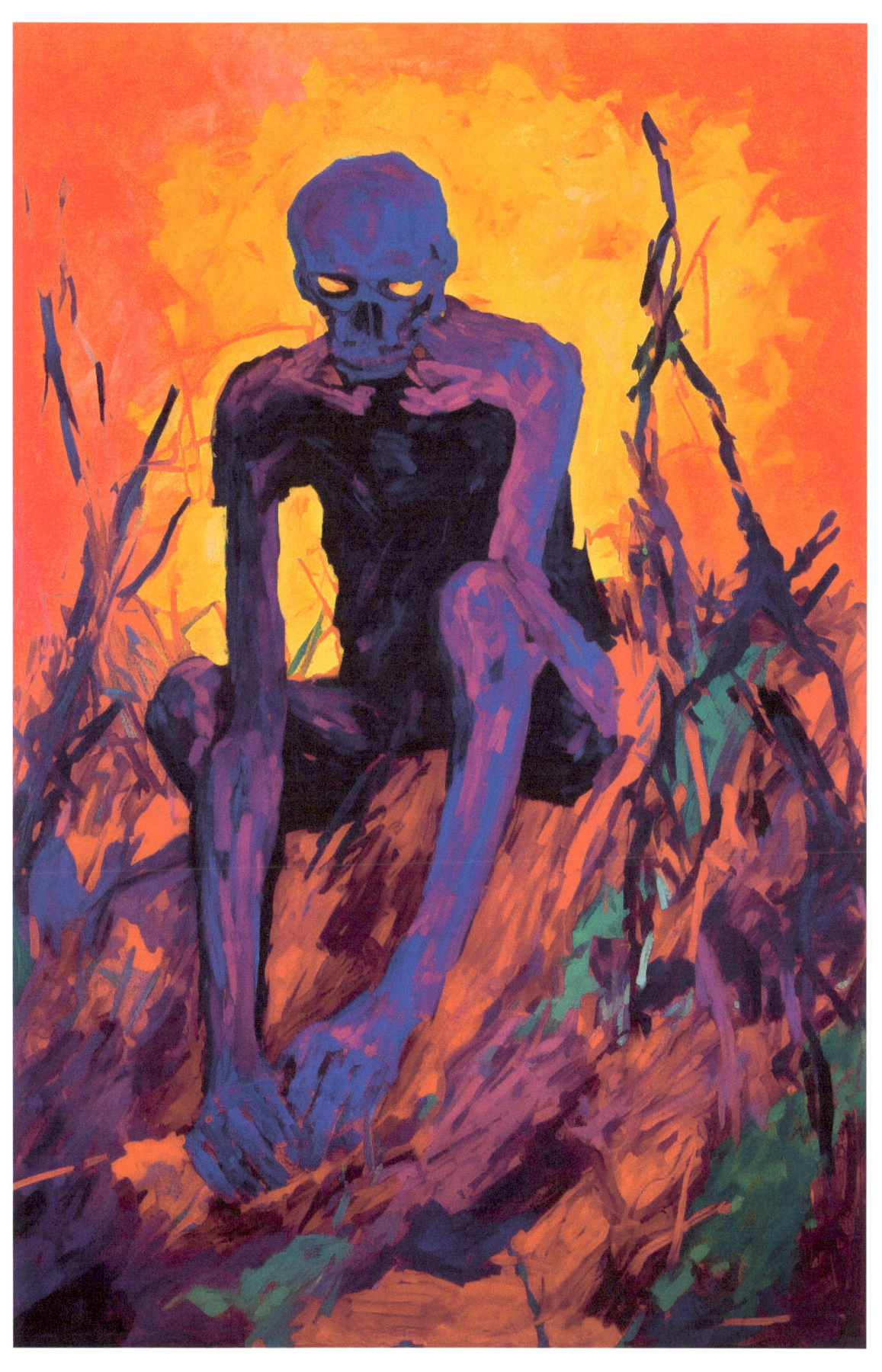

Cascade of Cadavers

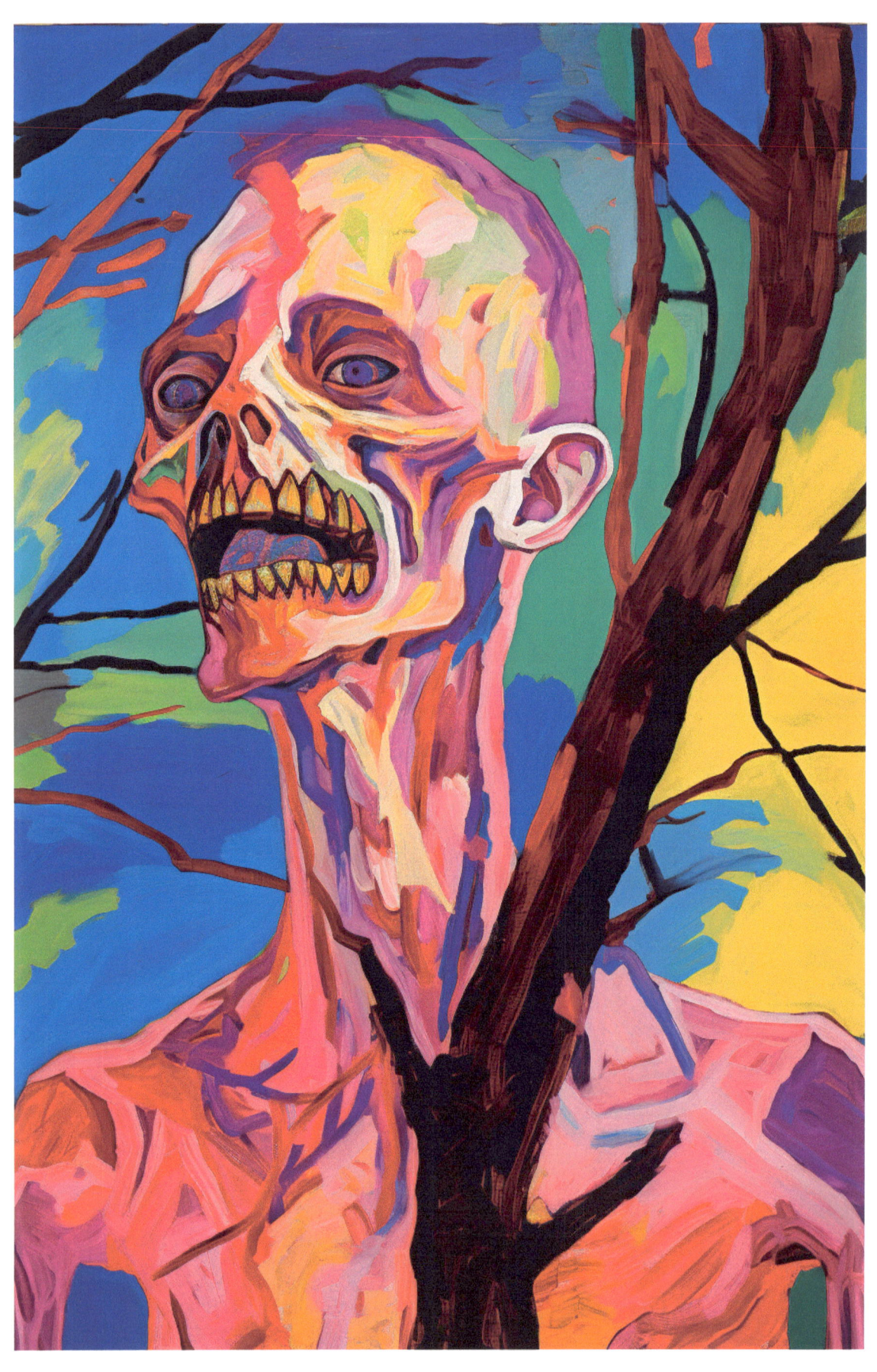

Frenzy of Fear

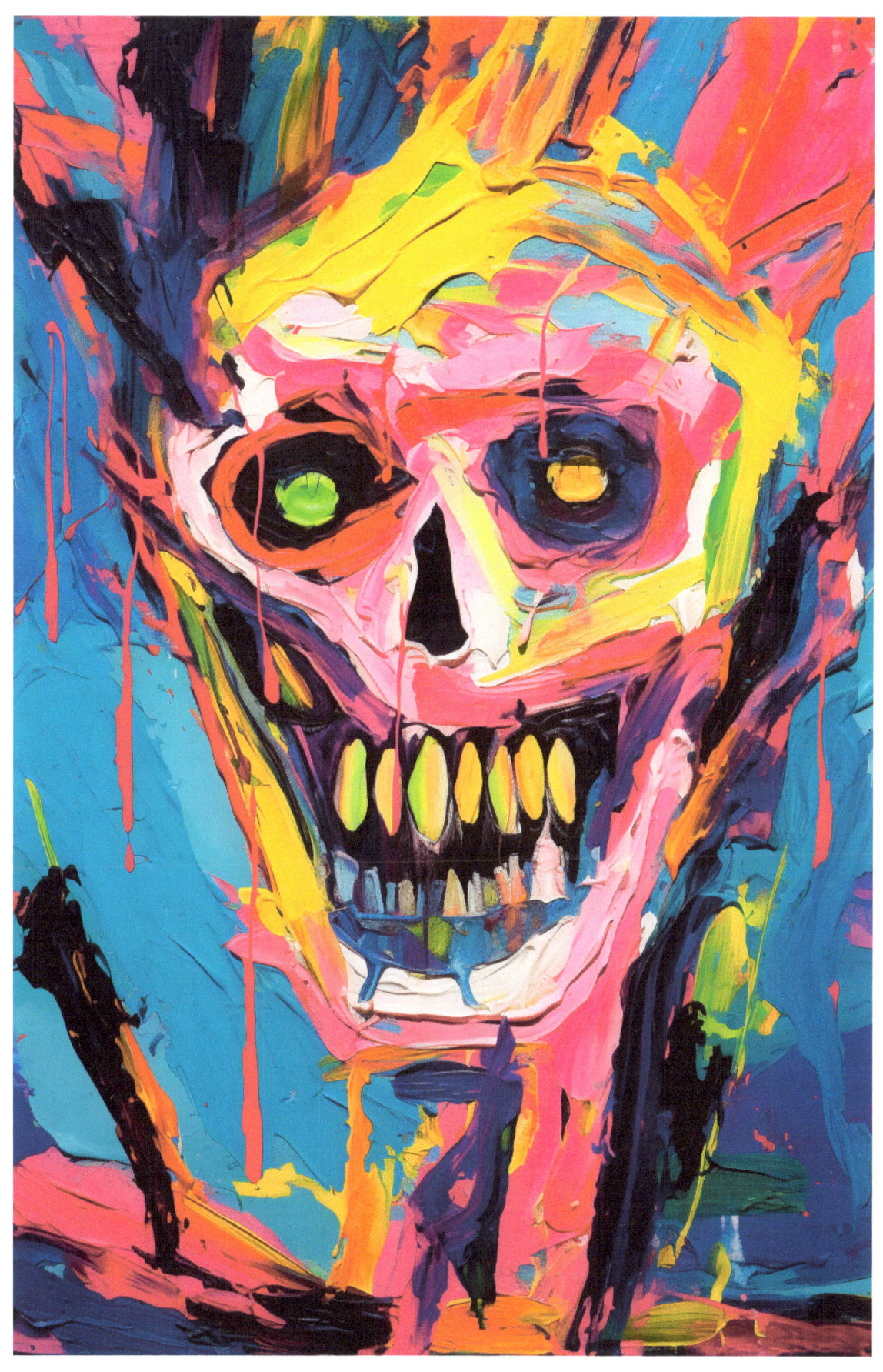

Rampage of Revenants

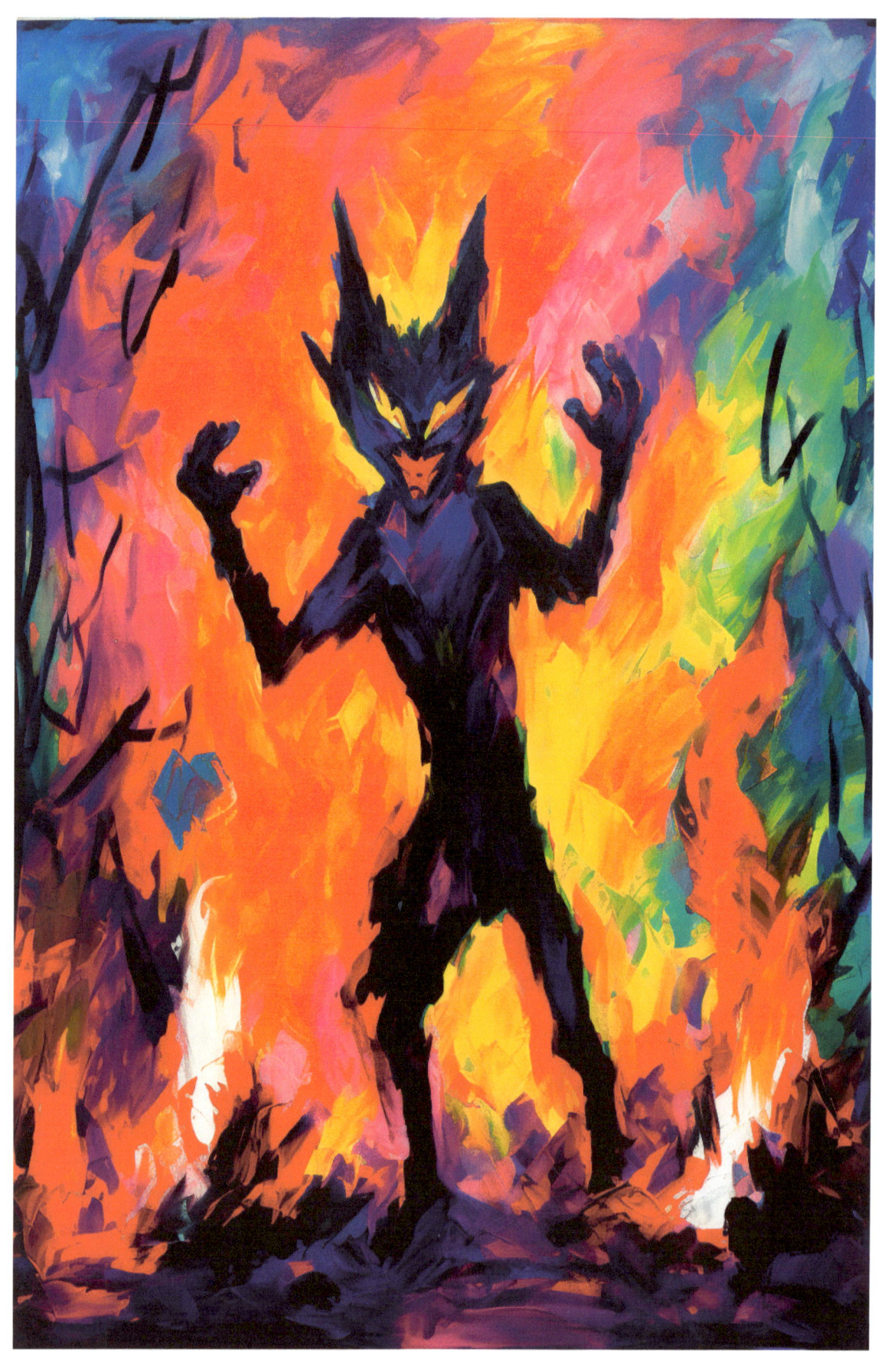

Squall of Screams

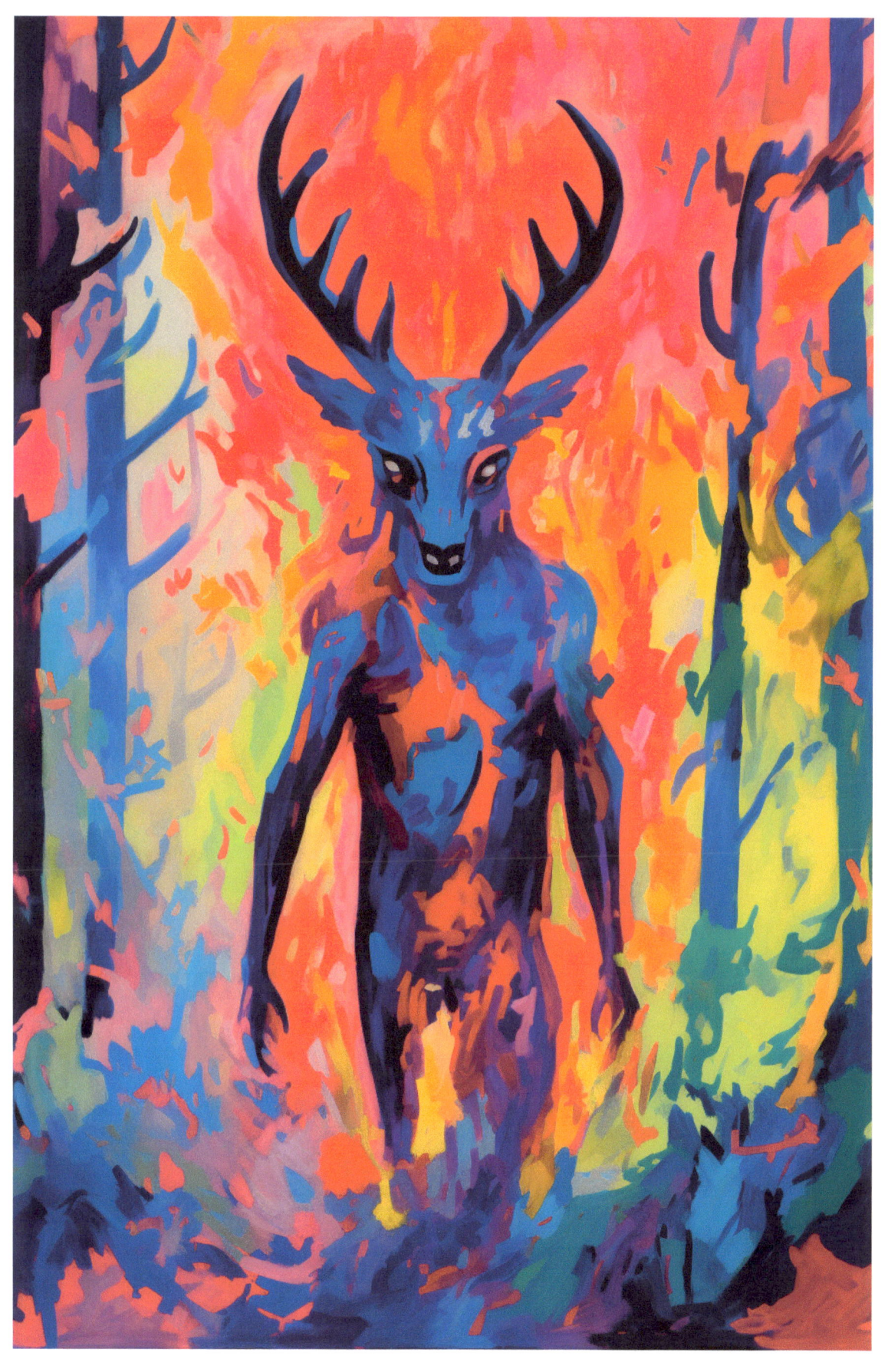

Tumult of Tombstones

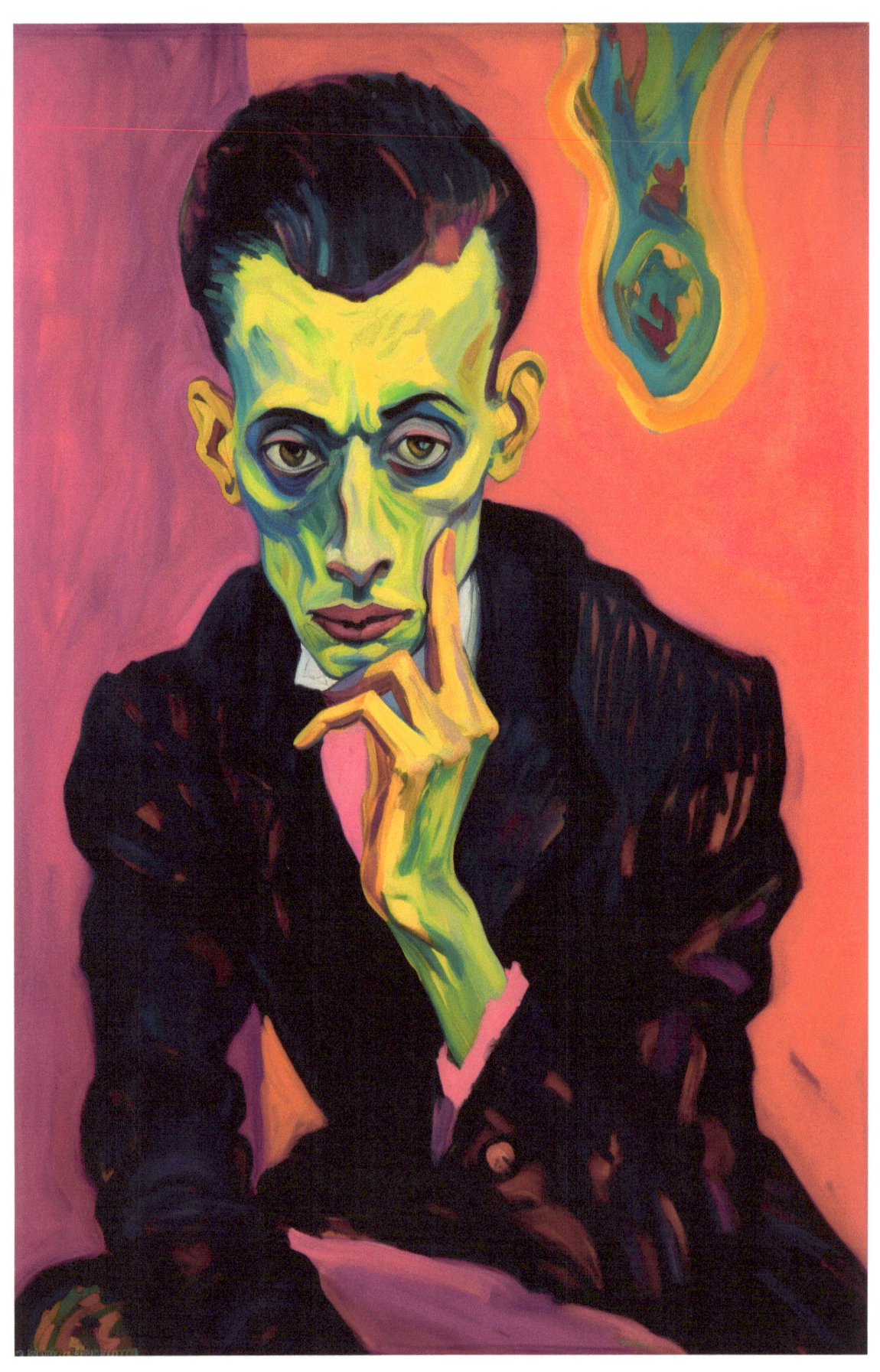

Torrent of Terrors

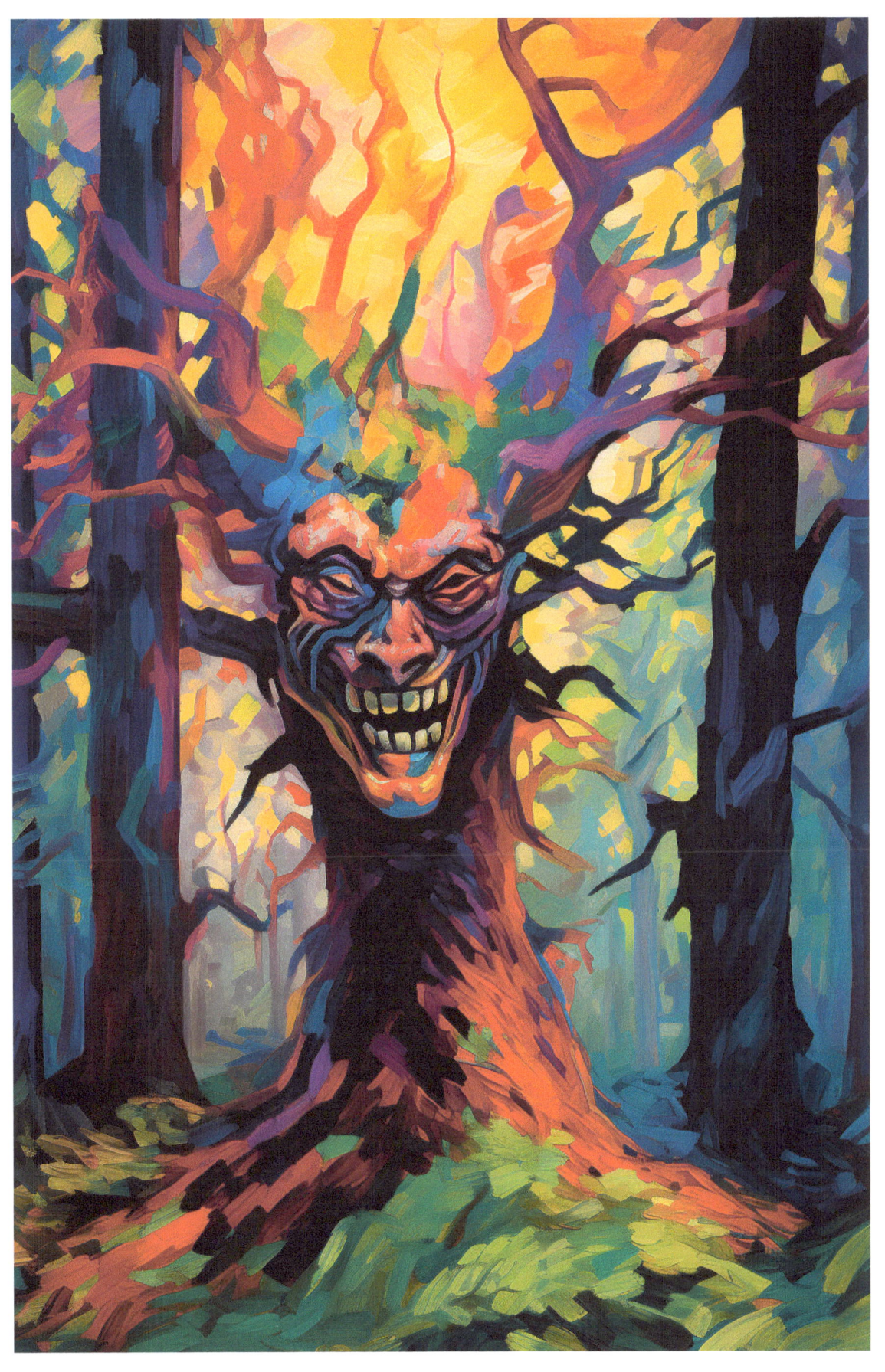

Storm of Spectres

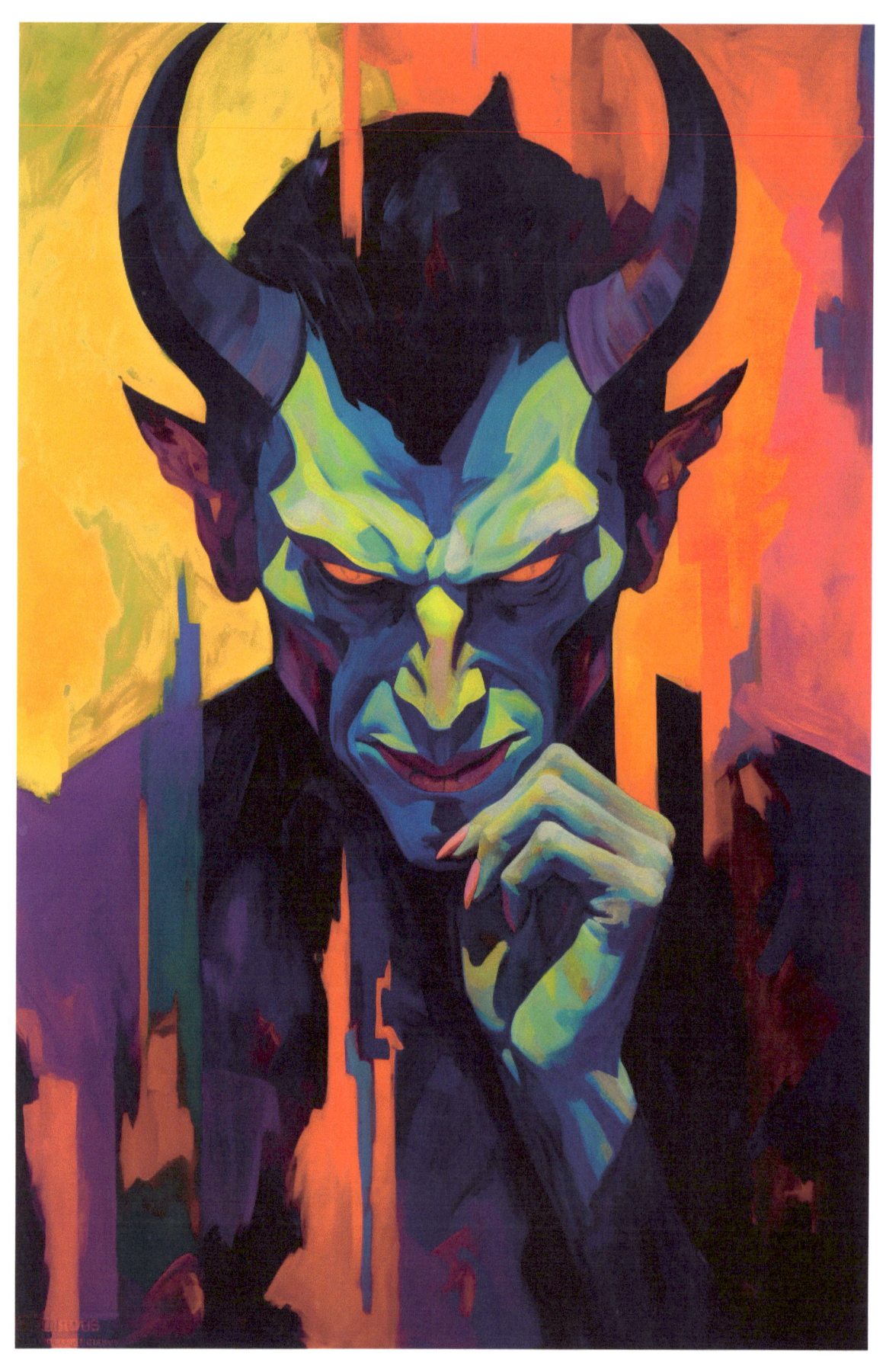

Rage of Ravagers

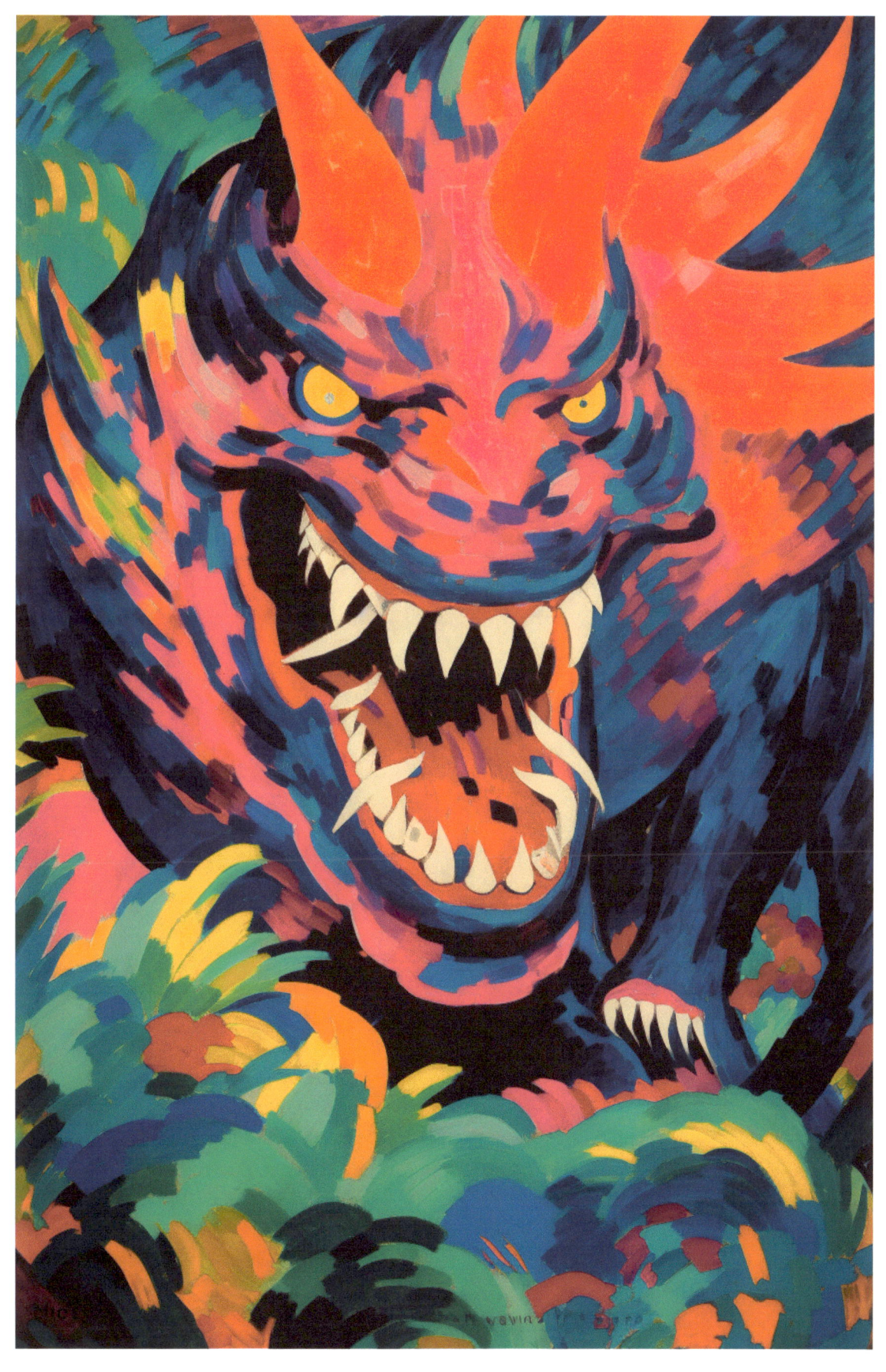

Vortex of Venom

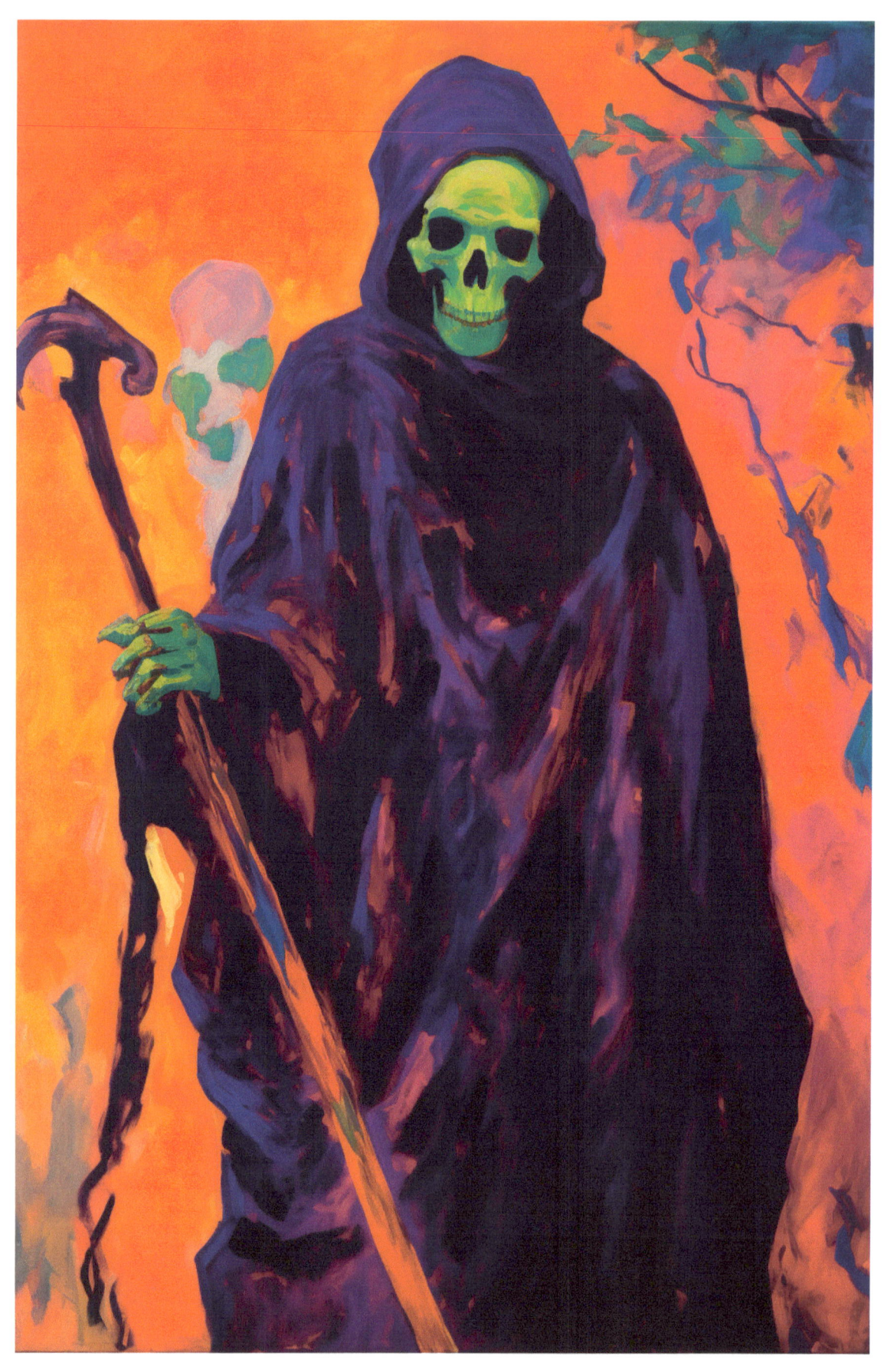

Cyclone of Caskets

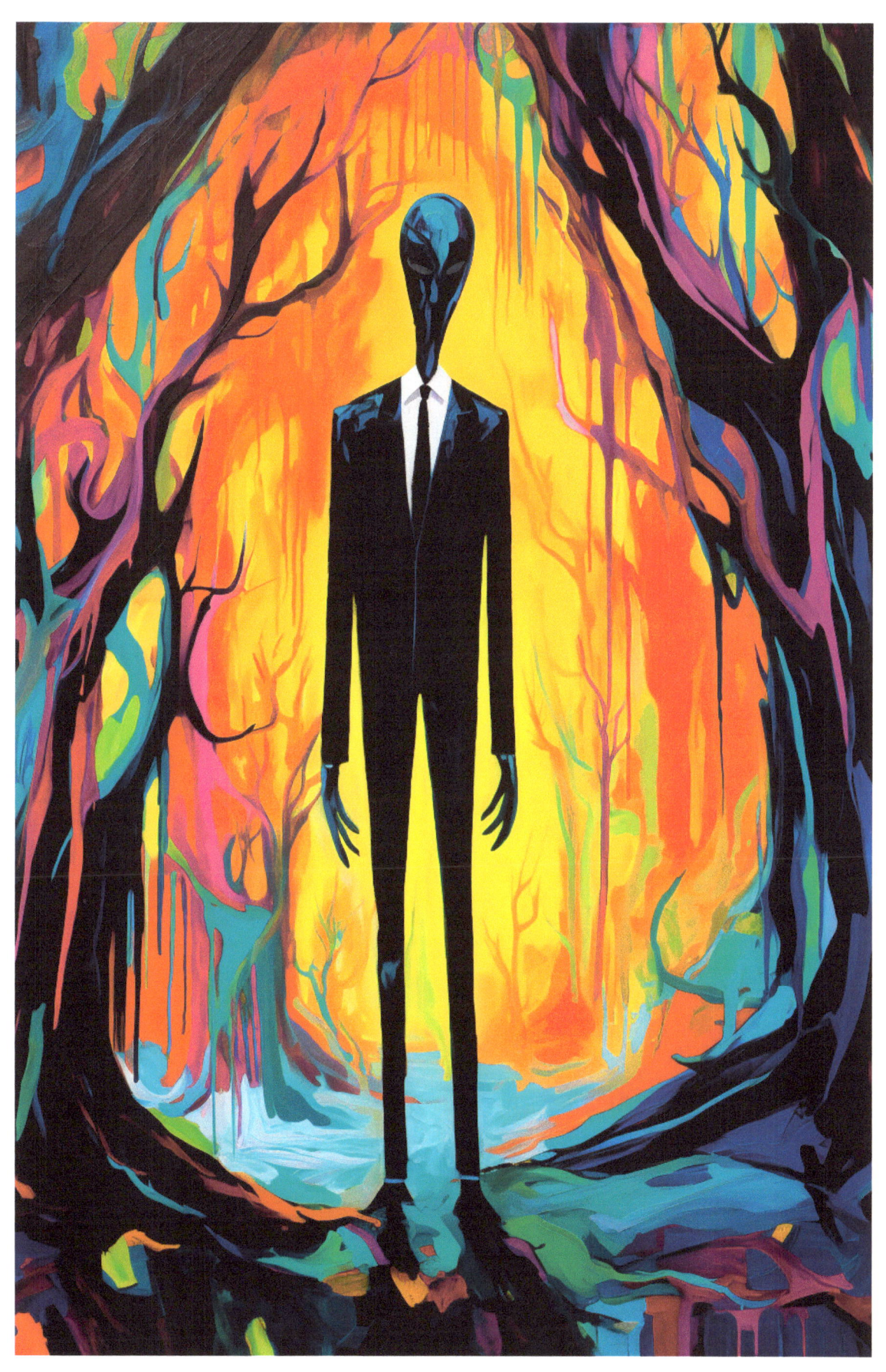

Elegy of Evil

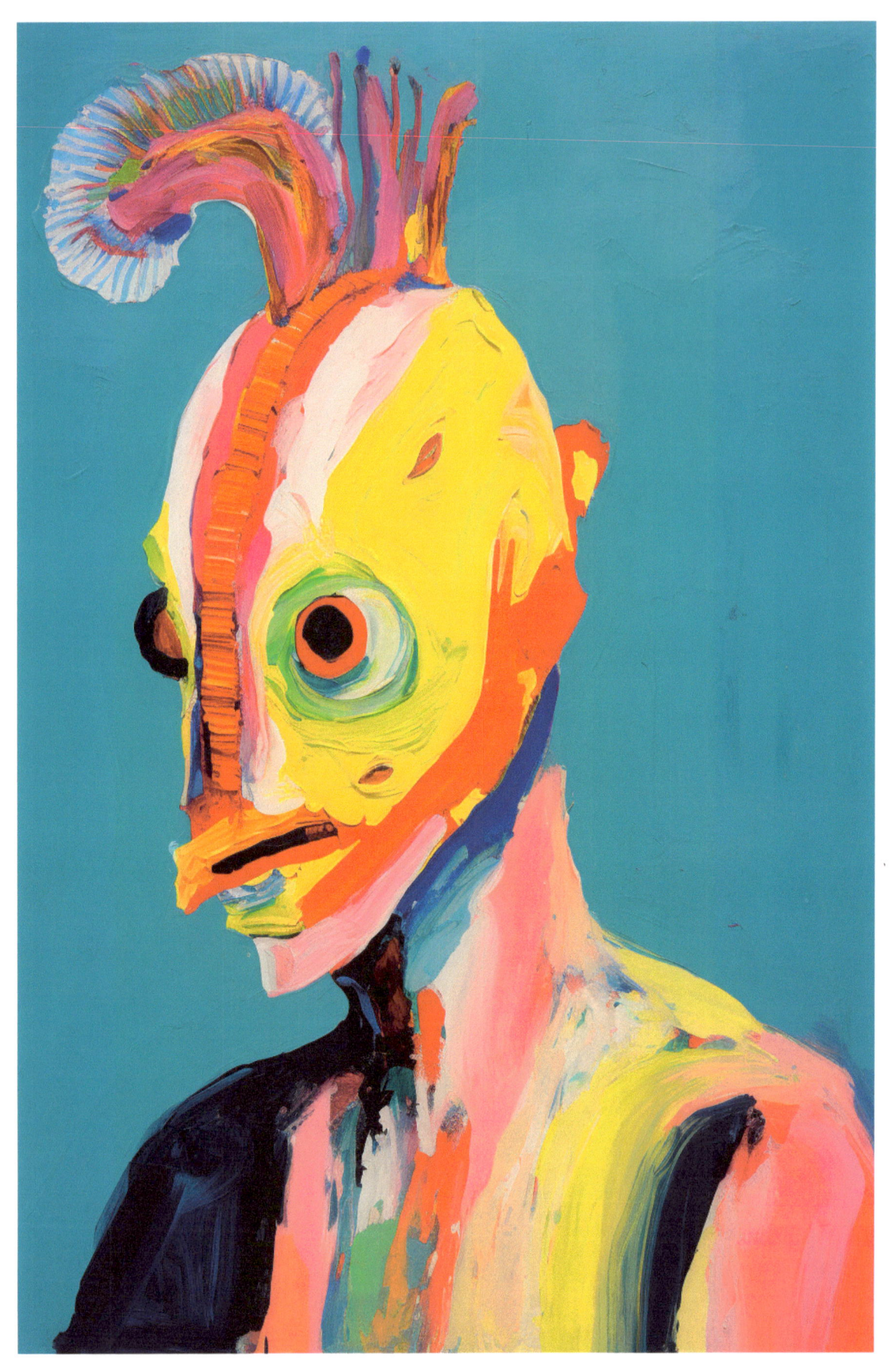

Tempest of Torment

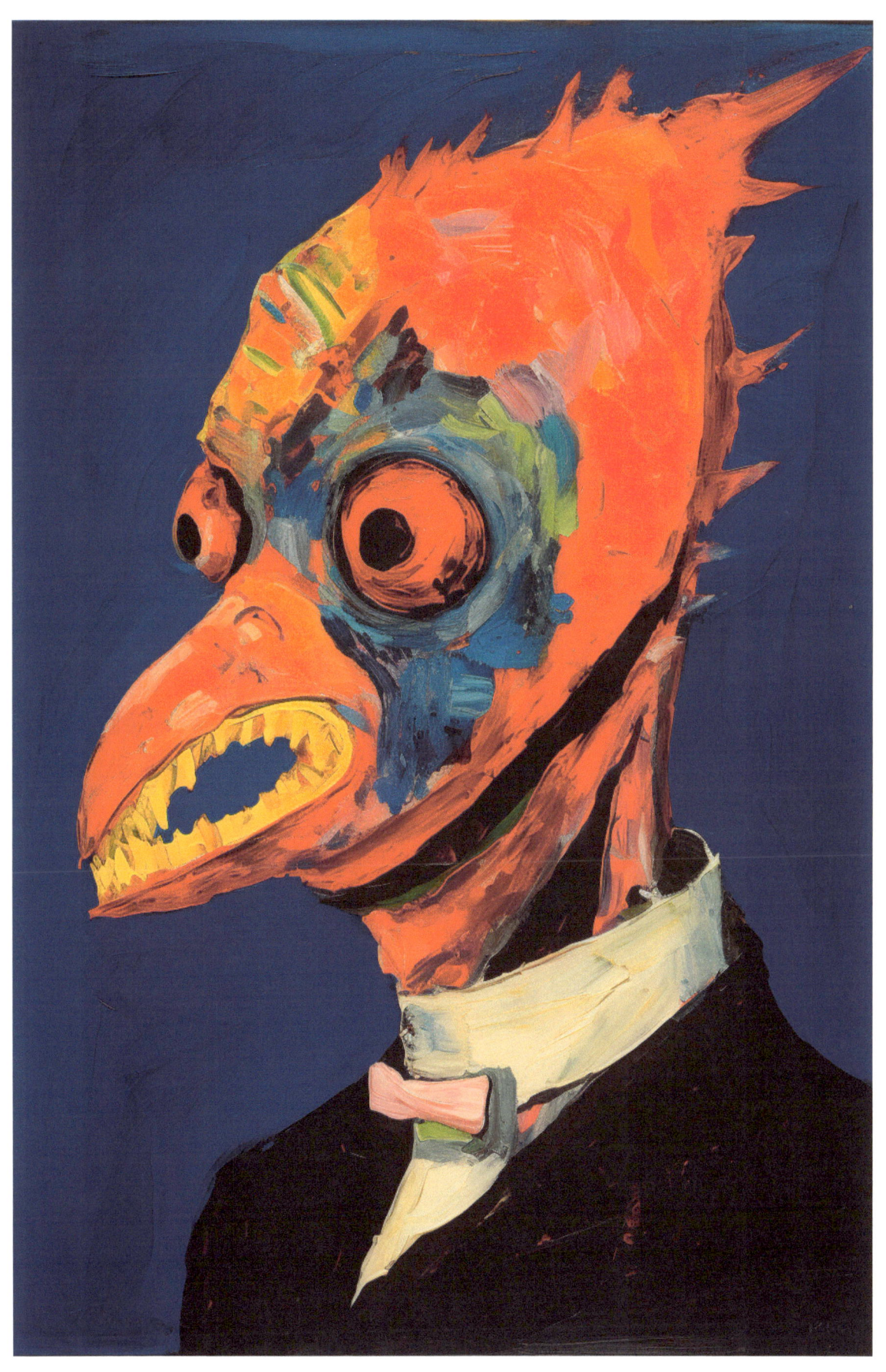

Flow of Fright

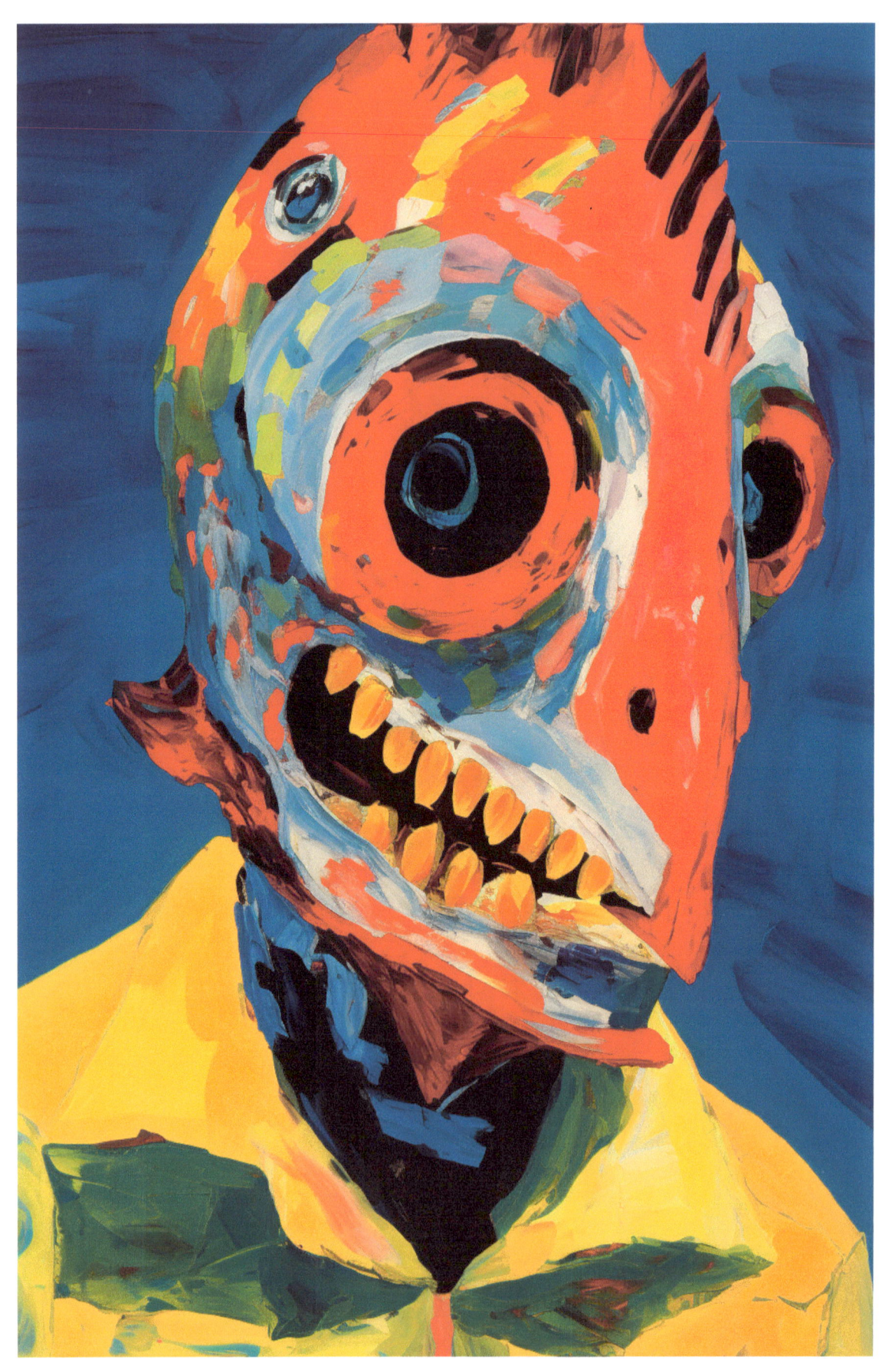

Rush of Rancor

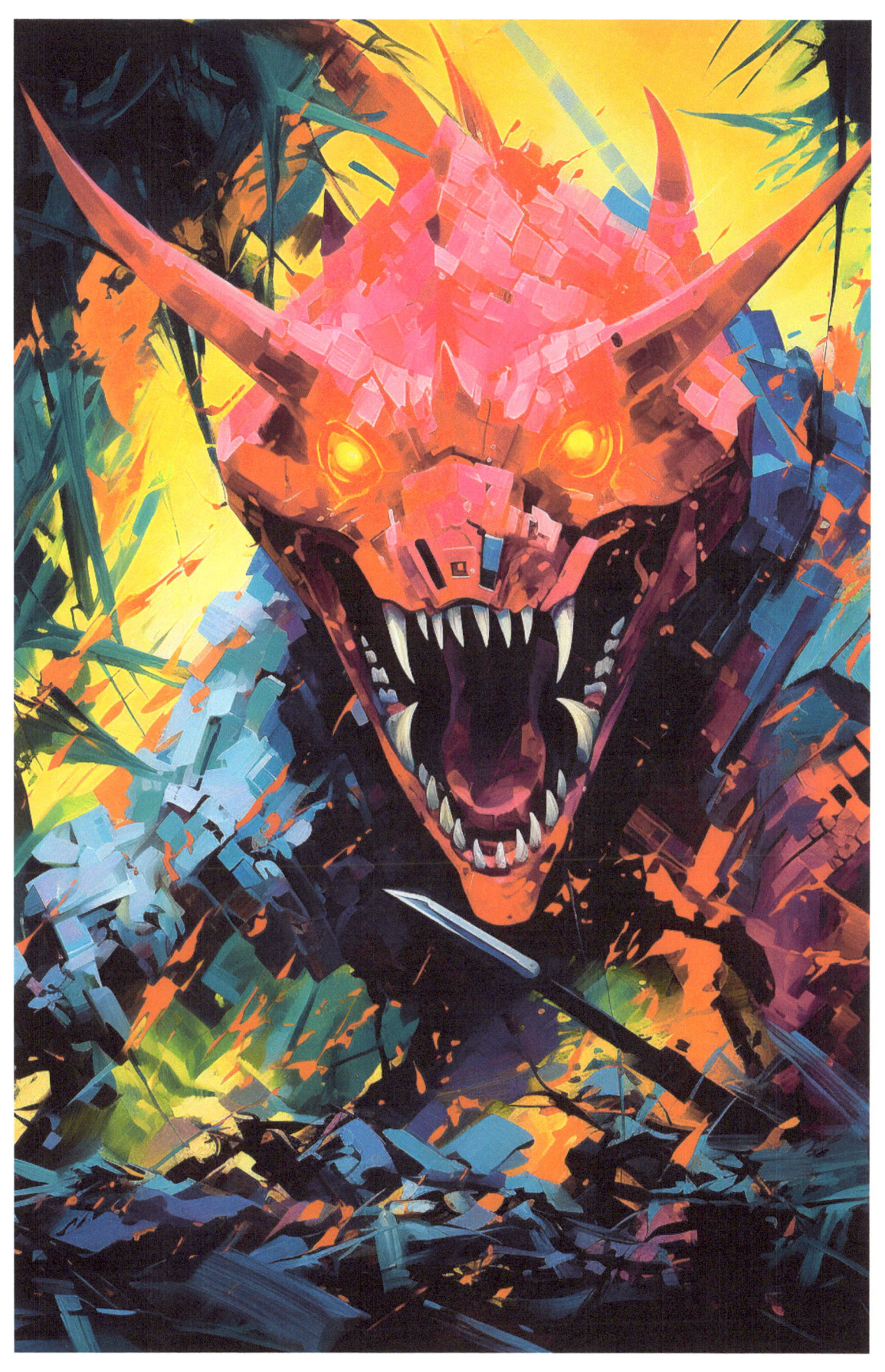

Avalanche of Agony

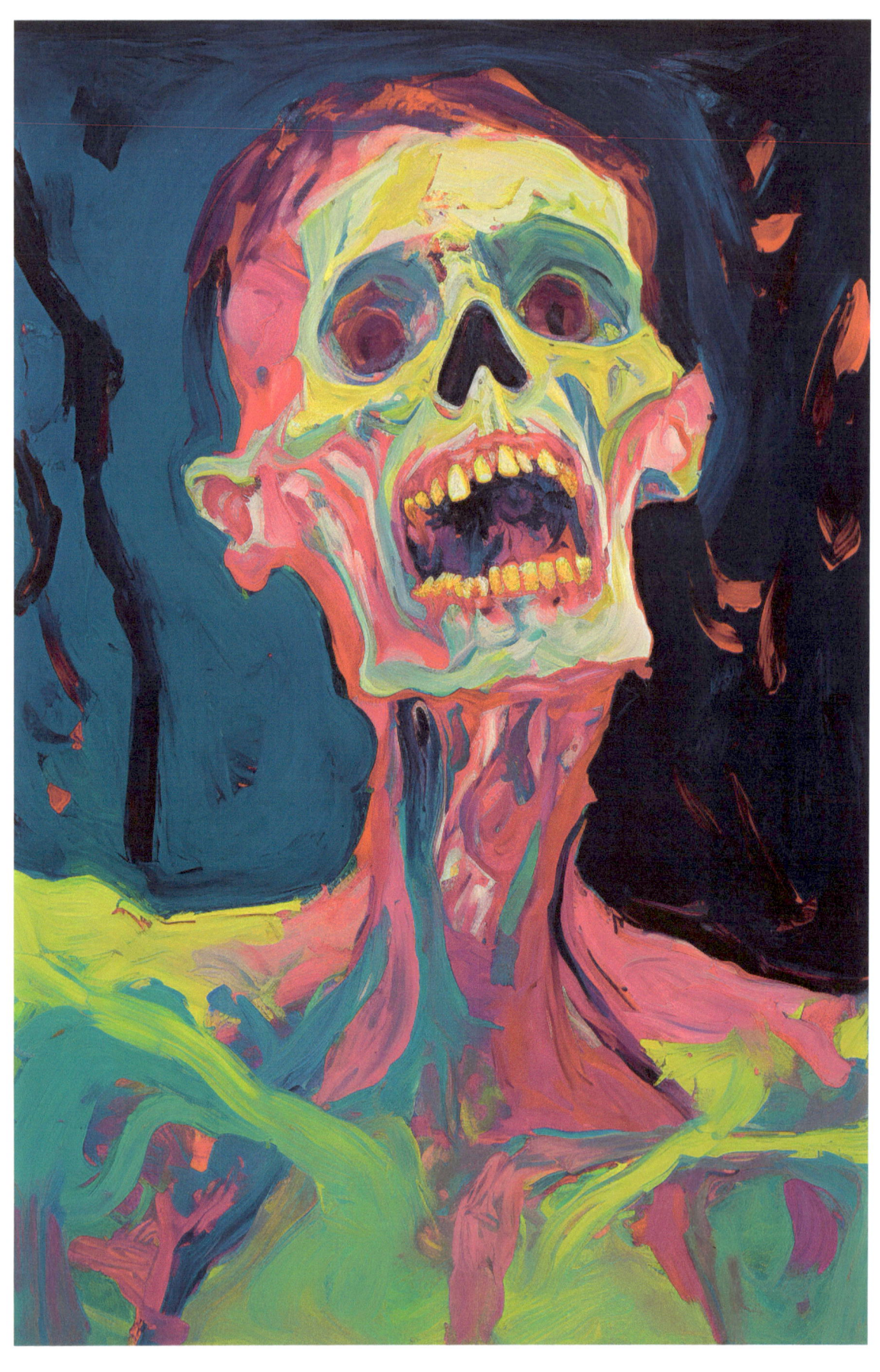

Flare of Fetters

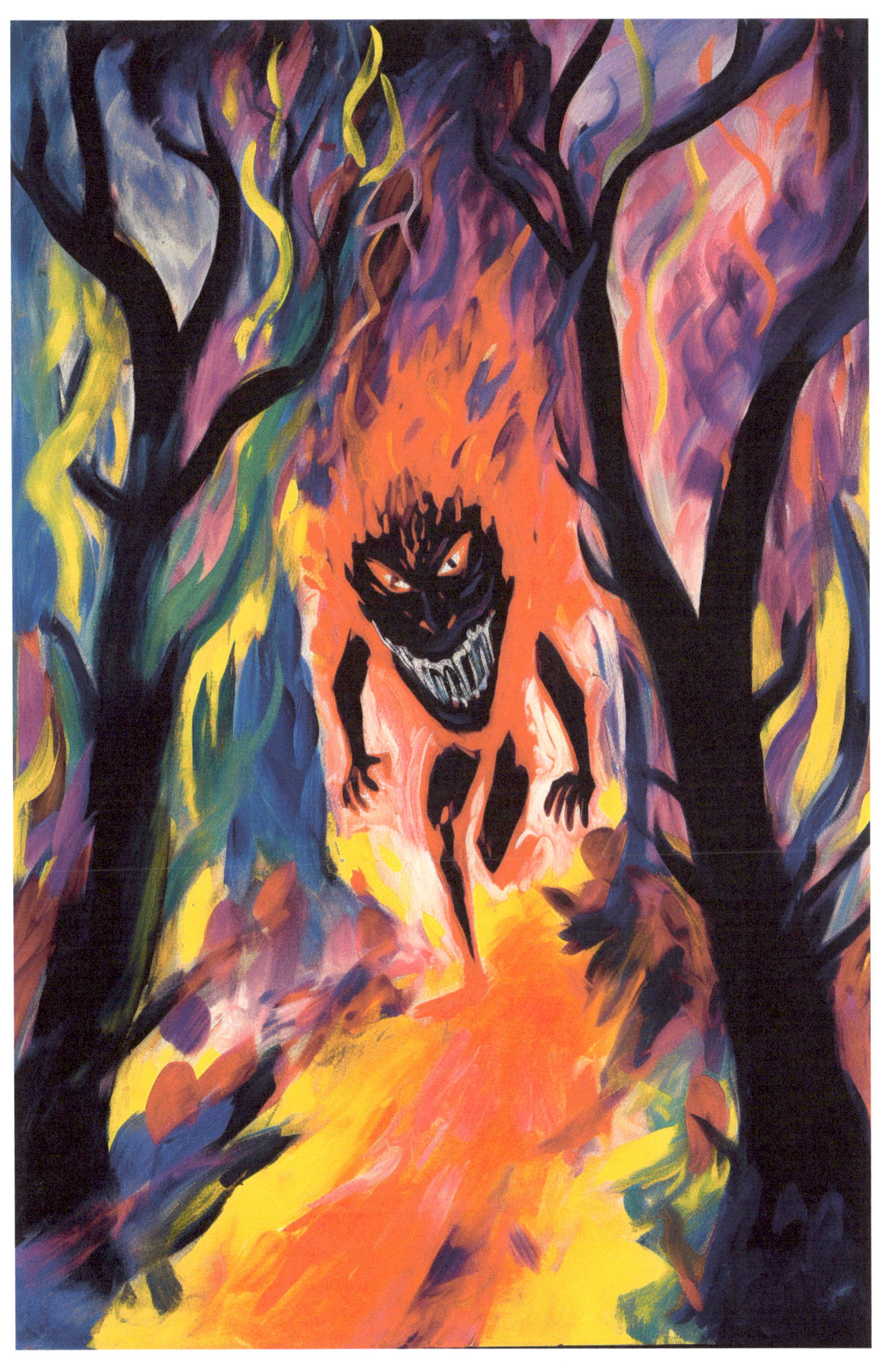

Rampant Restlessness

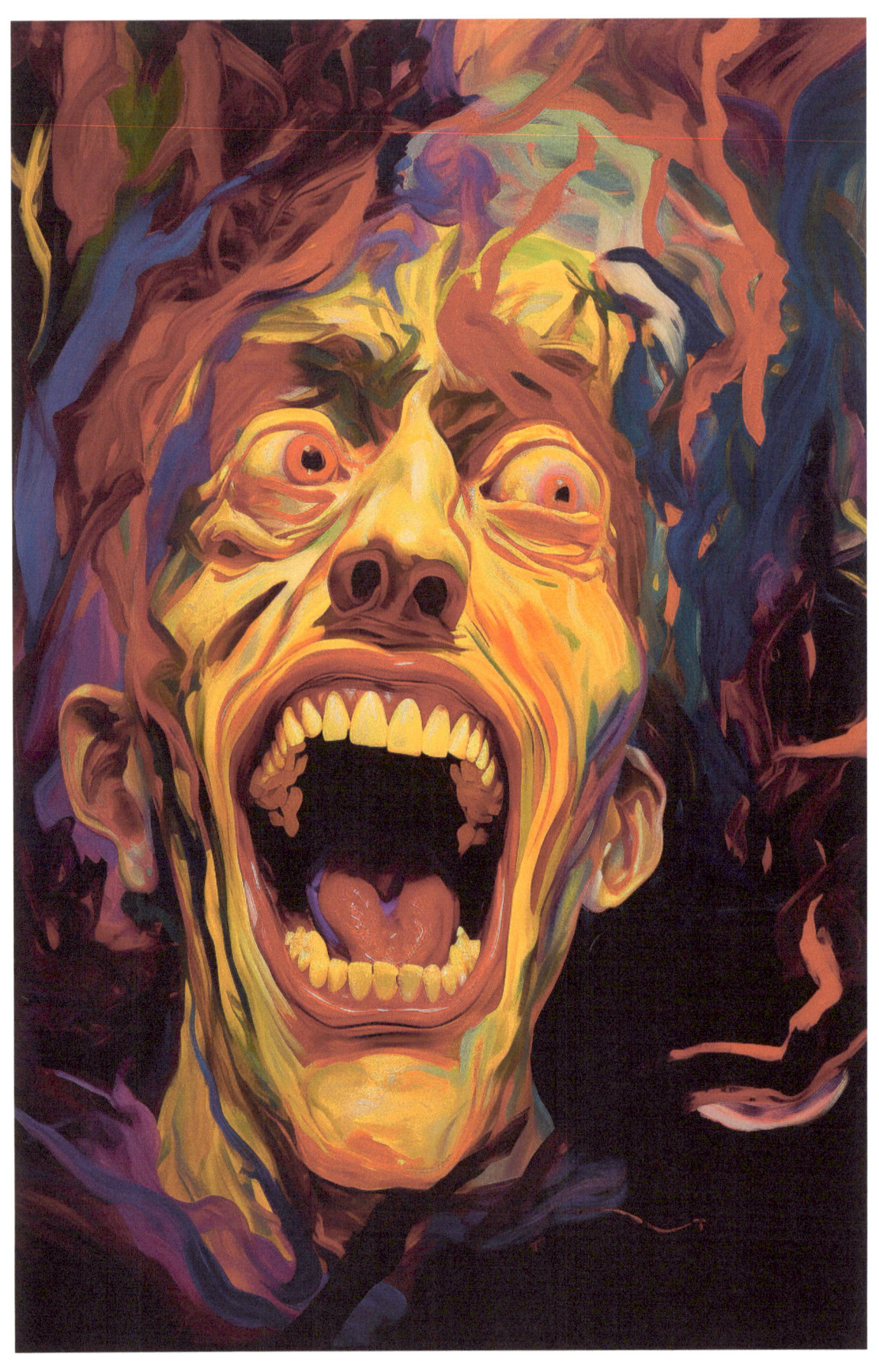

Riot of Reapers

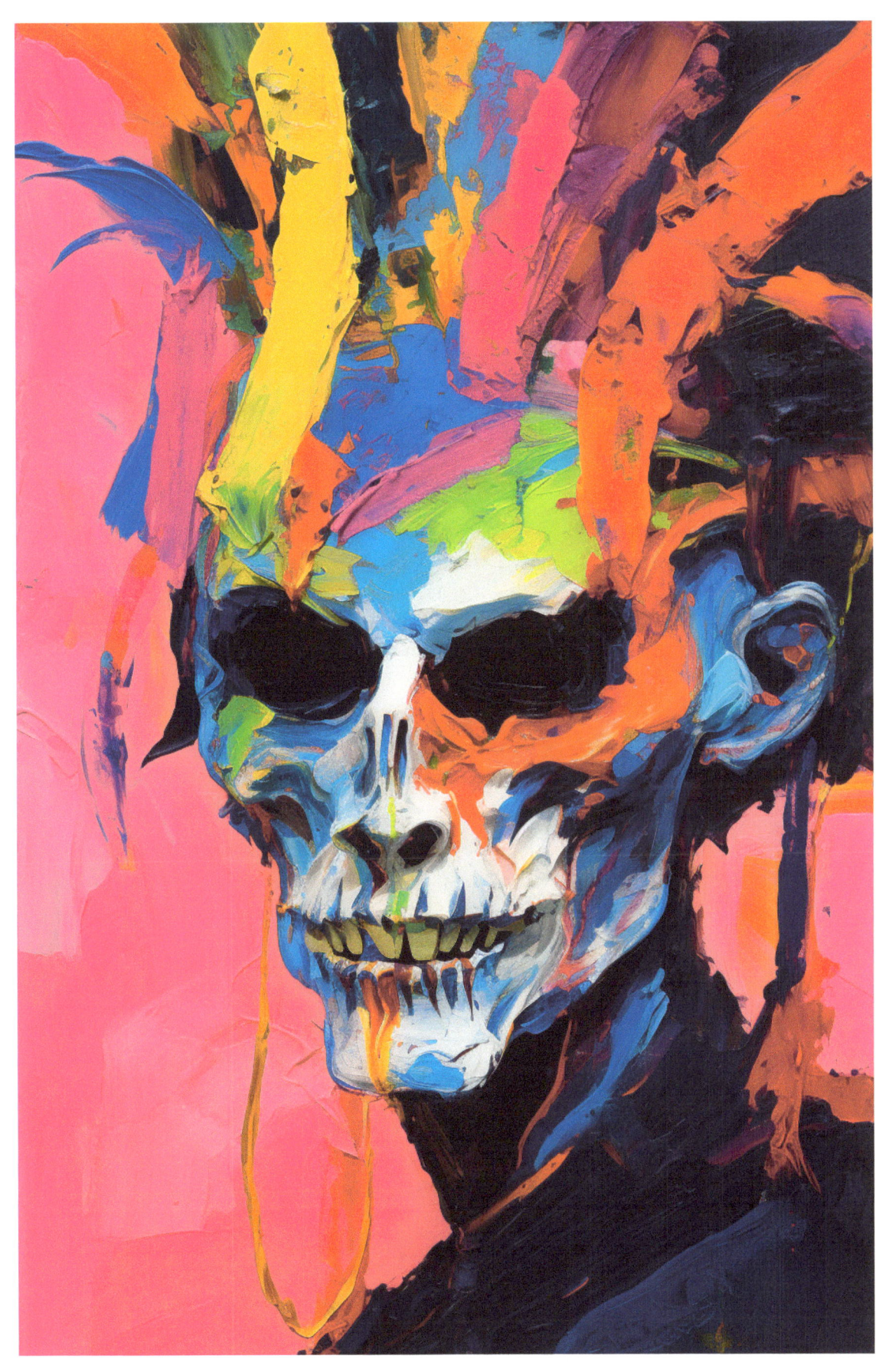

Chaos of Charnel

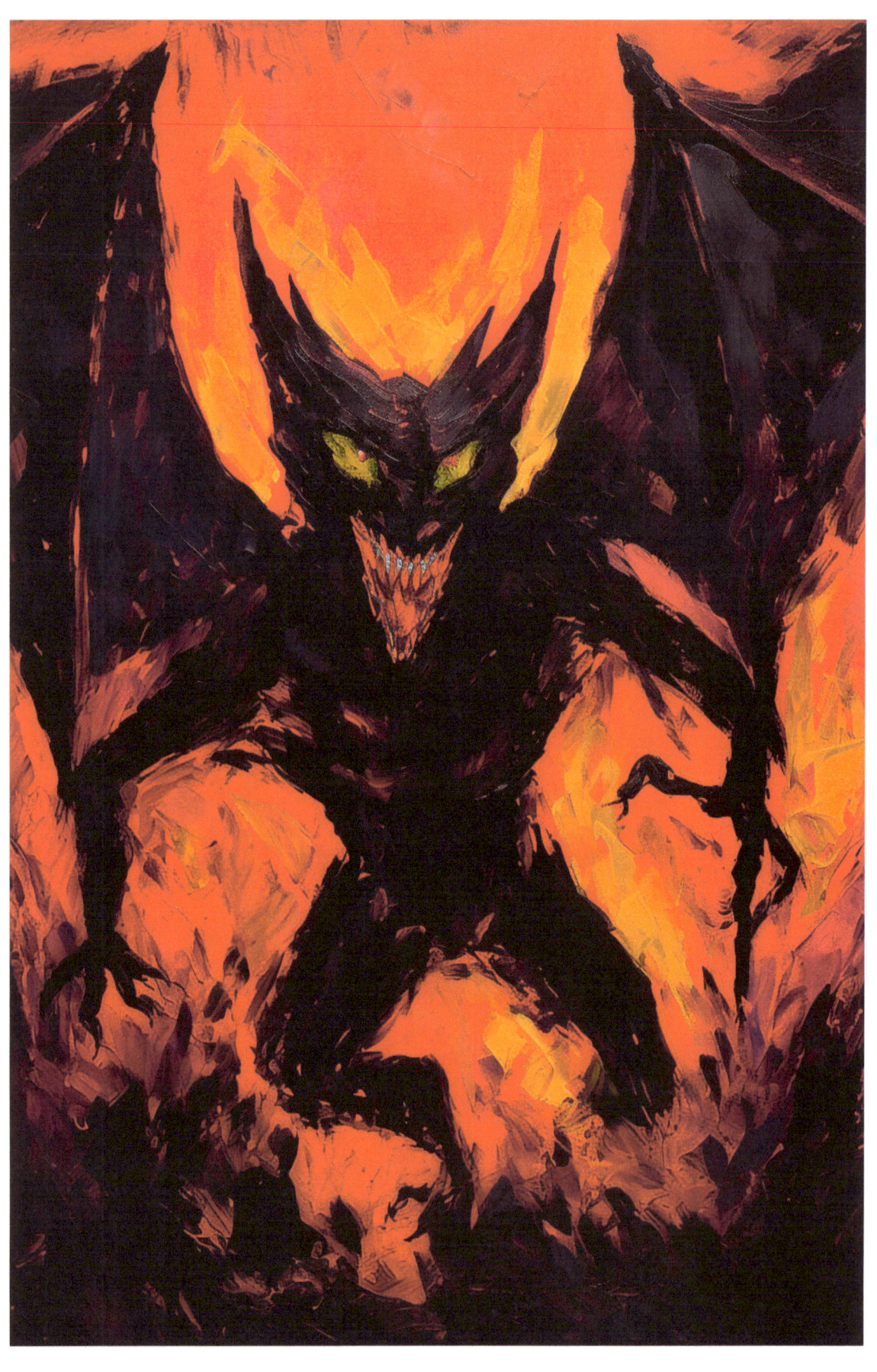

Maze of Maleficence

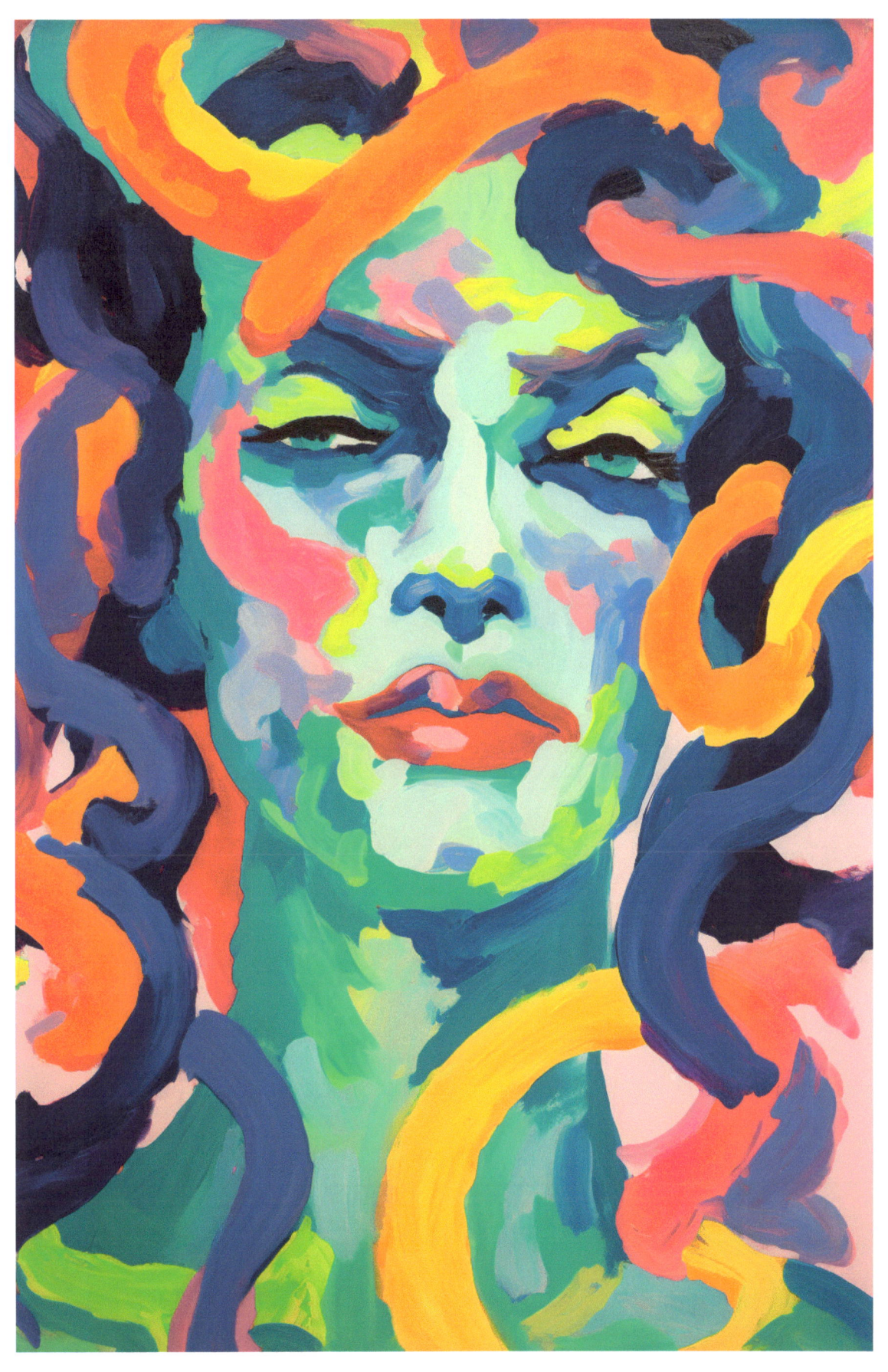

Blizzard of Banshees

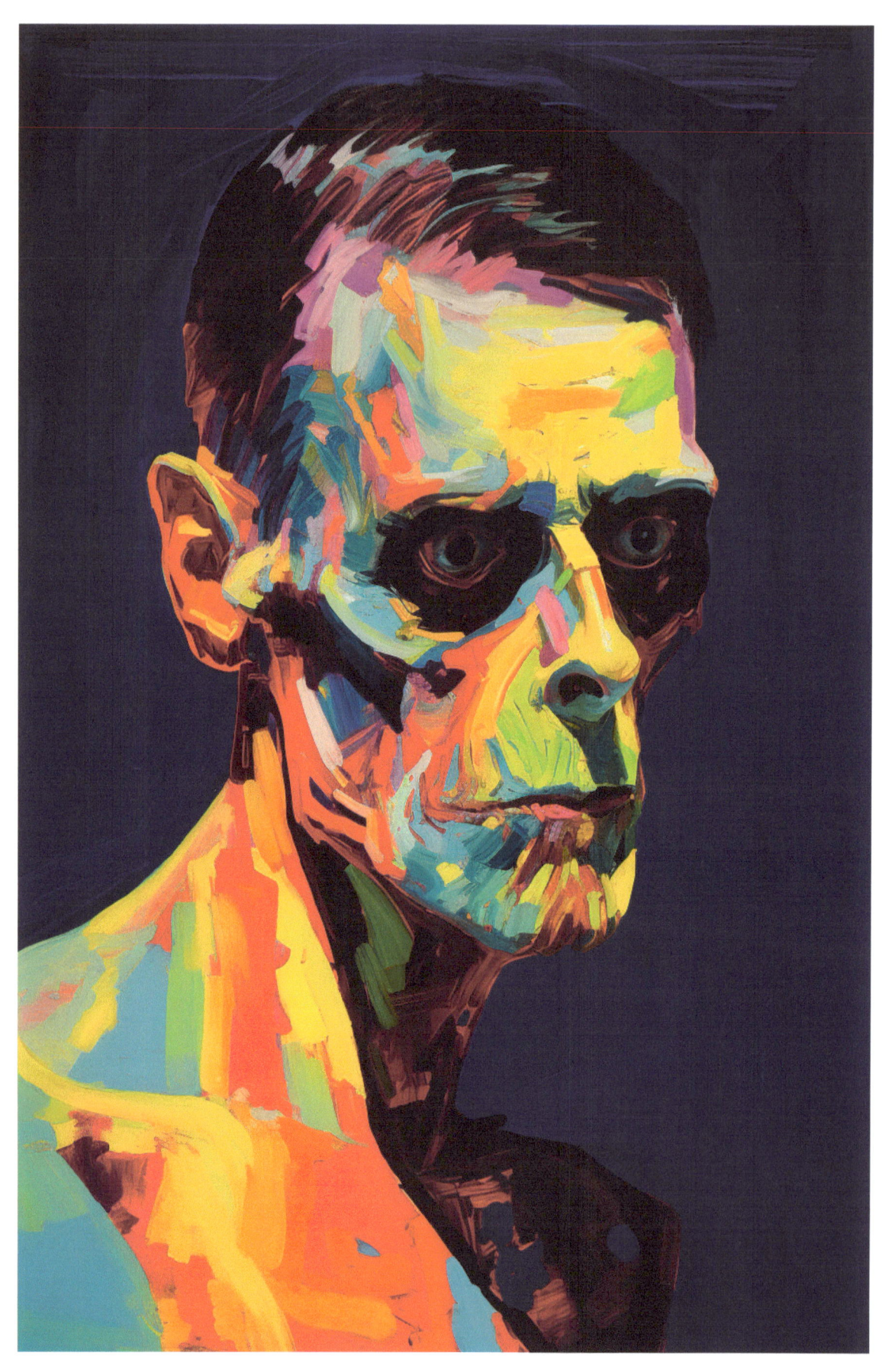

Maze of Maleficence

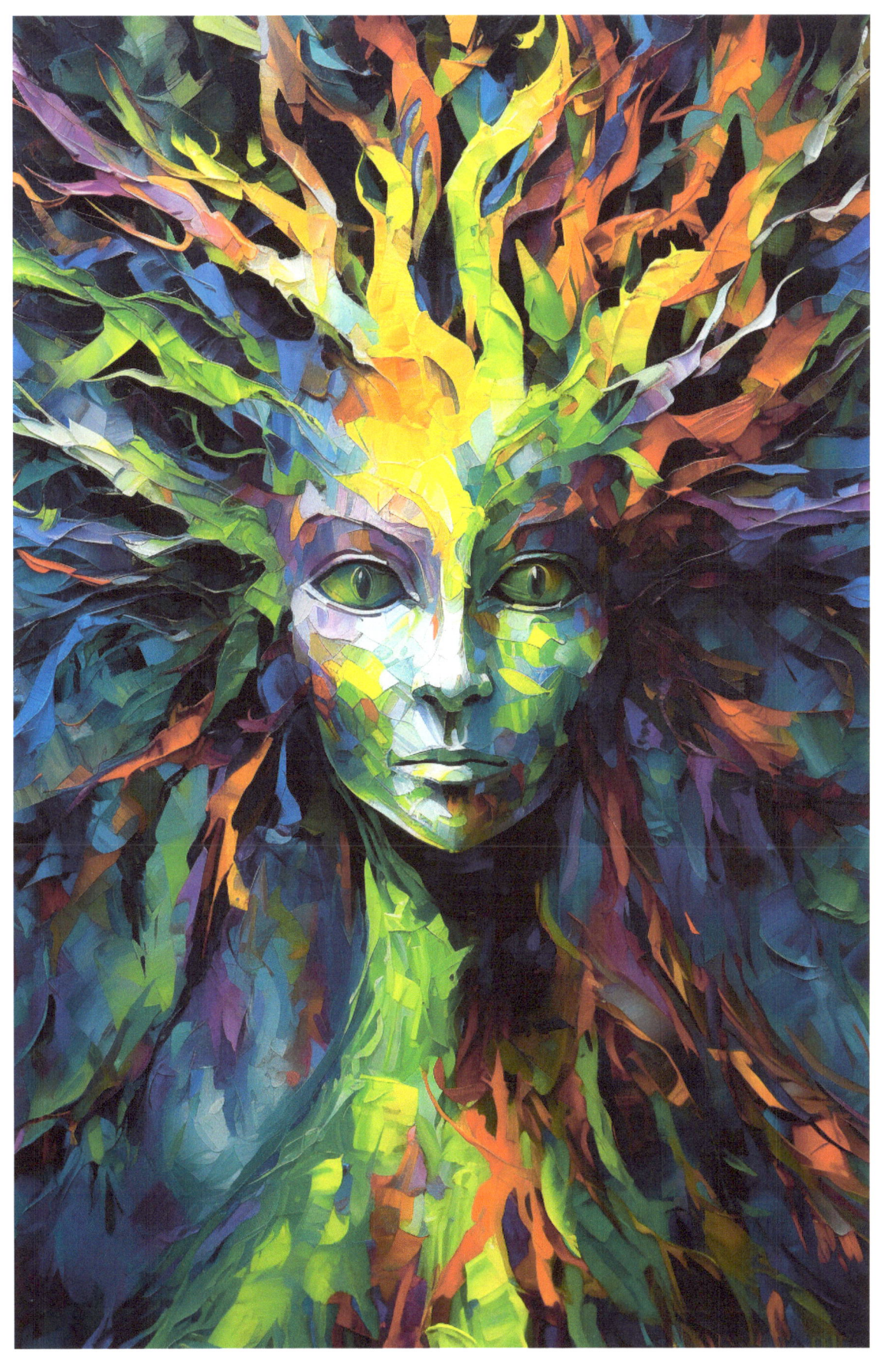

Winds of Wretchedness

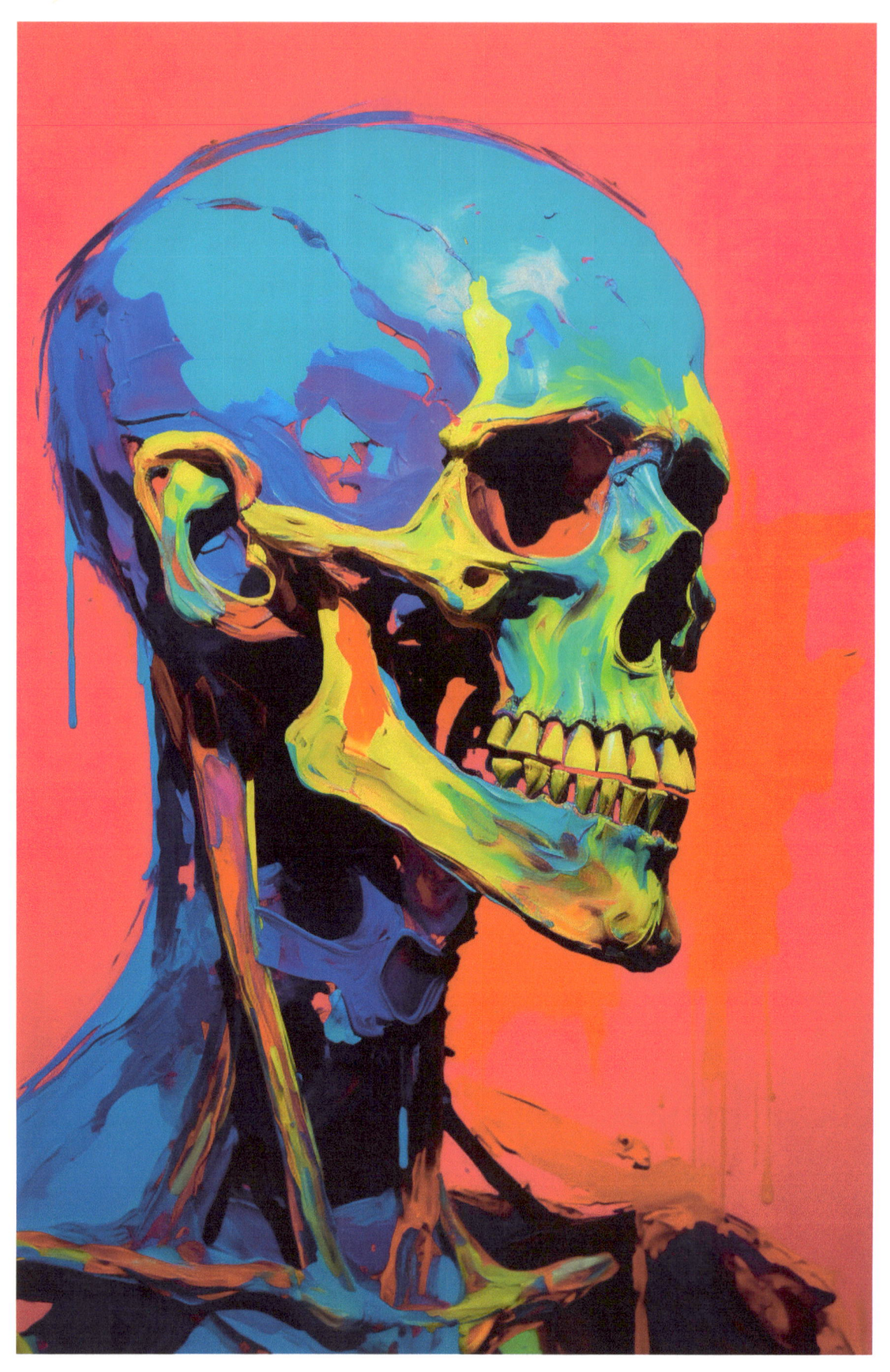

Spectral Surge of Suffering

Beautiful Beasties Prints